MSC Study Guide

Introductory Certificate - The APM Project Fundamentals Qualification (PFQ)

Published by Management Skills Centre Limited,

Registered Office:

Management Skills Centre Limited, Pantiles Chambers, 85 High Street, Tunbridge Wells, TN1 1XP

Paperback: ISBN: 978-0-9928841-2-3

Typeset in 11/14pt Meta OT
Printed and bound by Imprint Digital
Cover design by Fountainhead, Middlesex

MSC Study Guide

Introductory Certificate - The APM Project Fundamentals Qualification

Contents

Page No.	Topic

Preface

This Study Guide for the APM Project Fundamentals Qualification (PFQ) has four main objectives:

- To update previously used material in the light of the APM Body of Knowledge v6 (BoK 6) and the new syllabus for the APM Project Fundamentals Qualification.
- To ensure that the Study Guide complements the face-to-face sessions in a training course.
- To match the accompanying video podcasts and online examination to support distance learning.
- To encourage readers to use this as a stepping stone towards further APM Qualifications such as the APM Project Management Qualification (PMQ).

This Study Guide is divided into twenty-five topics which cover the whole syllabus - delegates can then use the Study Guide to shape their own pattern of learning. Each topic is linked to a podcast. The order in which the topics are taken differs from that in the syllabus to make a more coherent approach - see Appendix 2 for details.

We believe it important to ensure that any theoretical ideas are related to experimental data. So we have made our training relevant to the challenges now being faced by Project Managers. During classroom training sessions, it is particularly important to relate the topics to individual areas of interest for delegates, whether they be in construction, bio-science, engineering, IT, the arts or not-for-profit projects. It is the new problems being faced by delegates that make the sessions so interesting.

The primary objective of the training course and this Study Guide is to equip the delegates to pass the examination. So the 60 questions in the APM Sample Paper (April 2014) are discussed - they are listed at the end of the appropriate topic and may be found in Appendix 3.

Acknowledgements

I would like to thank the following:

- Berenice Meier and Heather Corrie for proof reading and editing.
- All our past delegates who through their searching questions have pushed me to keep clarifying and defining more carefully the concepts in this Study Guide.
- The Association for Project Management for permission to quote from various of its publications.

Any remaining omissions and errors are mine. All feedback to improve the content will be gratefully received.

Dedication

I dedicate this study guide to the memory of my physics teacher at Birkenhead School, Harold McCready. He introduced me via stage management for plays or pageants to various aspects of project management including scheduling. The preparation of a schedule leading to 'curtain up' was excellent training for developing a few years later at the European rocket range in Northern Sweden, a countdown to rocket launch for experimental measurements of the upper atmosphere. The project scientist's desk at ESRANGE was laid out in the same way as the stage manager's backstage control desk - communication switches and red/green cue lights to radar, launch, telemetry rather than to lighting, sound, front-of-house. Whatever the project, the fundamental principles remain much the same - an apt illustration of the importance of this Project Fundamentals qualification.

Andrew Scott
Tunbridge Wells
August 2015

Chapter 1 - Introduction to the course

During the course we emphasise the importance of clarifying the aims and objectives for all projects. So this must be the first task to be carried out.

Aims

The course is specifically designed to provide delegates with overall project management knowledge, skills and expertise.

At completion they will understand the language of project management and the structure of a successful project.

Objectives or learning outcomes

To describe and explain the 61 assessment criteria in the APM Course Syllabus.

To provide delegates with the knowledge and understanding such that they have the tools to pass the Examination - the first rung on the ladder of the APM Professional Qualifications.

Benefit

The benefit that comes after completion of the course, is that successful delegates will be able to take a more active part in a project team and make positive contributions to any project environment. Delegates have to ensure that this benefit is realised.

Teaching methods

23 video podcasts lasting a total of 148 minutes are freely available on the Management Skills Centre website - http://www.managementskillscentre.co.uk. These are MP4 files which allow one to listen to the trainer and see the slides to which he is referring.

Participants will be prepared for an examination based on the syllabus for the *APM Project Fundamentals Qualification* which is aligned to the *APM Body of Knowledge 6th edition*.

Taking the examination

The examination consists of 60 multiple-choice questions which must be attempted in one hour. Candidates have to select one out of four potential answers. This examination may be paper-based or on-line at the end of a training course. The online version may also be taken at home or the office using a proctor who monitors your behaviour during the examination using a web camera - often incorporated in a laptop. Thus both course and examination may be taken by self-study.

The pass mark is 60% i.e. you have to achieve 36 correct answers (or alternatively you are allowed up to 24 incorrect answers). The pass rate is currently over 90% of candidates.

There are two main ways of tackling the questions - either aim directly for the correct answer or eliminate incorrect answers leaving only the correct answer.

This is a very logical examination. The answers are often based on definitions. Try to use logic rather than feelings in your selections and read all the potential solutions to the question before selecting your answer.

If you are left with two potential answers, avoid guessing the correct solution - this is rarely successful. If you are not sure, just be consistent in your selection - the first or last of the two answers.

Benefits

During the course you may find a topic of particular interest and wish to introduce it into your work. Do highlight or underline in your notes (or the Study Guide); otherwise you will probably forget.

When the course is over, do try and write a plan for those actions you want to implement. Treat these changes as projects. Note also that changes to behaviour or culture take time and need careful monitoring and follow-up to succeed.

Chapter 2 - Projects and project management

Assessment Criteria - assessment will require a learner to demonstrate that they can:

1.1 define a project

1.2 identify the differences between a project and business-as-usual

1.3 define project management

1.4 state the key purpose of project management

1.5 list the core components of project management

1.6 list the benefits to an organisation of effective project management

2.1 Introduction

Firstly, we consider how projects may be managed - individually or grouped together within a programme or a portfolio. This topic may be called **P3 management**.

Project, programme and portfolio (P3) management is concerned with managing discrete packages of work to achieve objectives. (BoK 6)

First the word "objective" must be defined. The broad or general statement of the project's goal or aim or purpose may be distinguished from an objective which is more precise or, if possible, quantifiable.

We note that there are four types of objective - *Objectives may be expressed in terms of outputs, outcomes, benefits or strategic objectives. (BoK 6)*

1. Output = *the tangible or intangible product typically delivered by a project. (BoK 6)* e.g. a course study guide.

2. Outcome = *the changed circumstances or behaviour that results from the use of an output. (BoK 6)* e.g. the course study guide will allow training courses to be offered. Tutors must be trained to use the study guide and to be proficient in teaching the course. Changes to business-as-usual have to be implemented to take advantage of the outputs and generate the outcomes.

3. Benefit = *the quantifiable and measurable improvement resulting from completion of deliverables that is perceived as positive by a stakeholder. It will normally have a tangible value, expressed in monetary terms that will justify the investment. (BoK 6)* e.g.

the potential surplus resulting from running the new course that will contribute to the overheads of the business and to a profit.

A distinction is made that a benefit may be countable - as in the first part of the APM definition - or unaccountable ie just being an advantage; note the word 'normally' in the second sentence of the definition which acknowledges this alternative meaning. This recognises that many people ignore the precise meaning of the word objective and use the word to mean the same as a broad aim, goal or purpose.

4. Strategic objective = intermediary advances within the overall strategic plan in order to reach the strategic goal. e.g. The goal might be to offer a range of courses leading to professional qualifications. This course might be the second out of a target of five.

2.2 Projects

A project is a unique, transient endeavour, undertaken to achieve planned objectives, which could be defined in terms of outputs, outcomes or benefits. A project is usually deemed to be a success if it achieves the objectives according to their acceptance criteria, within an agreed timescale and budget. (BoK 6)

This is a very powerful definition because it clarifies why we do projects - to achieve their objectives.

Let us consider the plans for the new High Speed Two (HS2) rail network linking London to Birmingham, Manchester and Leeds, and allowing through-running trains to reach other cities (such as Liverpool).

In her speech of 10 January 2012 the Secretary of State for Transport, Justine Greening, said that, "The capital cost at 2011 prices of building the complete Y (-shaped) network is £32.7 billion. At present values, it will generate **benefits** of up to £47 billion and fare revenues of up to £34 billion over a 60-year period." Thus benefits will exceed costs.

The **output** is an approximately 540 km long railway line linking various cities and allowing trains to travel safely at up to 250 mph. It will be built in two phases - the first to the West Midlands by 2026, the second phase to extend northwards in two separate branches to Manchester and to Leeds by 2033. It will be built to a European structure gauge; this allows taller and wider rolling stock than the UK rail network.

So what are the **outcomes**? If we consider peak period fast trains departing or arriving at Euston station, it means that after completion of Phase 2, running 18 HS2 trains per hour out of a total of 30 trains per hour. (The Strategic case for HS2 - October 2013). Each 400m train is capable of carrying up to 1100 passengers; this gives a maximum of nearly 20,000 passengers per peak hour - many of whom access the underground tube lines. "Euston station currently handles a maximum flow of about 7,000 passengers per hour across the concourse to the Underground at peak periods. The introduction of high speed services may involve an additional 10,000 passengers per hour needing to access the Underground." - reported in the Evening Standard 28 February 2011. Clearly much expenditure is required to change the current arrangements to cope with the additional tube passengers. These costs to enable the outcomes to be achieved are part of the total project costs.

A report from the Department of Transport in March 2015 entitled 'HS2: on track' stated that its objectives were to:

- provide sufficient capacity to meet long term demand, and to improve resilience and reliability across the network; and
- improve connectivity by delivering better journey times and making travel easier.

Are these really objectives or just broad aims? There is a tendency to avoid precise objectives as it is then easier after the event to claim success. If I aim to lose weight - a loss of 1kg means I have been successful - unfortunately 1kg is not enough to have a meaningful effect!

2.3 Project Management

Organisations have existing structures for the ongoing and routine management of business-as-usual. Project management works across these structures drawing on the expertise and knowledge of the organisation as well as external third parties, if appropriate, to deliver a project.

Projects are usually initiated by one organisation and may be carried out by that organisation. However some of the work is often contracted out to other organisations; they may carry out their share of the project without obtaining an overall view of the project. In this study guide we are going to look at the project from the view of the initiating organisation, in order to see how the whole of the project is managed from start to finish.

Project management is the application of processes, methods, knowledge, skills and experience to achieve the project objectives. (BoK 6)

We must give examples of what these words mean to ensure the words are properly understood:

- process - a series of progressive stages such as the risk management process described in Chapter 9.
- method - an orderly and structured approach to project management, such as described in the procedures found for example in the PRINCE2 methodology.
- knowledge - what may be found in the APM Body of Knowledge.
- skills - practised ability to carry out aspects of project management e.g. using a software package such as Microsoft Project.
- experience - the result of prior acquaintance with using processes, methods, knowledge and skills to manage projects.

This definition of project management clarifies the purpose of project management - to achieve the project objectives.

Differences between Project and Business-as-usual and the implication for the way projects are managed. Note this list is not exhaustive.

Aspect	Projects	Business-as-usual	Implication for the way projects are managed
Uniqueness	Unique	Repetitive	Importance of new and different Project Management Plan (PMP) for each project
Timescale	Temporary	Ongoing	Limited lifetime demands schedule planning to enable control during implementation
Attitude to change	Seeks to introduce revolutionary change	Improves by evolutionary change	Importance of change management - the production of outcomes.
Deliverables	Delivered once	Repeated deliveries	Emphasis on getting it right first time; thus detailed planning required, e.g. how the required quality is to be achieved
Resources	Transient resources	Stable resources	Resource scheduling necessary as part of resource management

Aspect	Projects	Business-as-usual	Implication for the way projects are managed
Attitude to risk	Need to be risk aware	Tends to be risk averse	Risk management plan an essential part of the PMP

It is these differences that cause the special features of project management.

The core components of project management are:

- *defining the reason why a project is necessary;*
- *capturing project requirements, specifying quality of the deliverables, estimating resources and timescales;*
- *preparing a business case to justify the investment;*
- *securing corporate agreement and funding;*
- *developing and implementing a management plan for the project;*
- *leading and motivating the project delivery team;*
- *managing the risks, issues and changes on the project;*
- *monitoring progress against plan;*
- *managing the project budget;*
- *maintaining communications with stakeholders and the project organisation;*
- *provider management;*
- *closing the project in a controlled fashion when appropriate. (BoK 6)*

Effective project management is beneficial - there is a greater probability of achieving:

- the project objectives,
- an efficient and best value use of resources,
- satisfaction for the differing people or organisations involved with or affected by the project (stakeholders - see chapter 8).

A large project may be divided into sub-projects each with their own unique deliverables that contribute to the overall project deliverable e.g. Crossrail, with nine new stations each a project in its own right. It is possible for several projects to each produce their own unique deliverables, which then collectively contribute to a greater goal or benefit. Such projects are brought together under a programme and managed using programme management, which is discussed in the next chapter.

APM Sample Paper (see Appendix 3)

Questions - 14, 15, 29, 44, 45, 59

Chapter 3 - Programme and portfolio management

Assessment Criteria - assessment will require a learner to demonstrate that they can:

1.7 define programme and portfolio management and their relationship with project management

3.1 Programme Management

Work that combines projects with change management (ie outputs plus outcomes) to deliver benefits is considered to be a programme.

Programme management is the coordinated management of projects and change management activities to achieve beneficial change. (BoK 6)

"Characteristics of programmes:

- *Their purpose is to deliver the capability to make strategic, significant or step changes to organisations, normally referred to as or measured by benefits.*
- *This need for significant improvement will be consistent with the organisation's strategy, and programmes will help to deliver elements of that strategy.*
- *The creation of the desired benefits will be achieved only through the co-ordination and successful completion of a number of component projects.*
- *Different parts of an organisation or differing organisations may be affected by the programme.*
- *The overall measure of success will be determined by the actual delivery of the expected benefits, which frequently involves the use of capabilities or facilities created by the programme in an ongoing, 'business-as-usual' manner." (APM Introduction to Programme Management - 2007)*

This is important because it clarifies what aspects of the management of projects are carried out at programme management level and are thus not usually the responsibility of a project manager. The project manager has to deliver an output that is capable of delivering the required benefits but is not responsible for realising those benefits.

The core programme management processes are:

- *project coordination: identifying, initiating, accelerating, decelerating, redefining and terminating projects within the programme. Managing inter-dependencies between projects, and between projects and business-as-usual activities;*
- *transformation: taking project outputs and managing change within business-as-usual so that outputs deliver outcomes;*
- *benefits management: defining, quantifying, measuring and monitoring benefits;*
- *stakeholder management and communications: ensuring that relationships are developed and maintained, thus enabling productive, two-way communication with all key stakeholders.*

Responsibility for these components lies with three key roles within programme management: a programme sponsor, a programme manager and business change managers.

- *The sponsor is accountable for achievement of the business case and providing senior-level commitment to the programme.*
- *The programme manager is responsible for day-to-day management of the programme including the coordination of projects and change management activities.*
- *Business change managers are responsible for successful transition and benefits realisation." (BoK 6)*

By way of example, a project might be the construction of a warehouse. When additional projects such as a computerised stock-control system and staff training are added it becomes a programme which delivers the capability of supplying customers faster, with reduced costs and less wastage due to goods damaged in transit. The challenges for the project manager are linked to understanding those aspects of the programme that impinge on the project.

3.2 Portfolio Management

A collection of projects and programmes designed to achieve strategic objectives is called a portfolio.

Portfolio management is the selection, prioritisation and control of an organisation's projects and programmes in line with its strategic objectives and capacity to deliver. The goal is to balance change initiatives and business-as-usual while optimising return on investment. (BoK 6)

Some organisations may have one portfolio - all their projects and programmes. Larger organisations may have multiple portfolios relating to geography, subsidiaries or operating division.

An example of the use of portfolio management is for projects and programmes in new product development (NPD) and Research and Development (R&D). An example from a County Council is the Cabinet member given a portfolio such as Education.

Portfolio management addresses three questions to the portfolio:

- Are these the projects and programmes needed to deliver the strategic objectives, subject to risk, resource constraints and affordability?
- Is the organisation delivering them effectively and efficiently?
- Are the full potential benefits from the organisation's investment being realised?

The following techniques may be used:

- strategic planning;
- change management;
- project and programme management.

Portfolio management involves the following:

- segmenting the portfolio into categories and tailoring the investment criteria accordingly;
- portfolio prioritisation based on assessments of risk and return;
- assessment of progress via stage gates;

- periodic portfolio-level reviews and regular portfolio reporting;
- consistent portfolio-wide approaches to benefits management.

There are regular reviews to review the balance of investment and benefit or risk and reward, creating and closing projects and programmes as necessary. This will include termination before completion.

Organisations seek a mixture of projects and programme that fulfill their strategic objectives. When a fixed resource pool has to be shared amongst a number of projects and programmes some form of prioritisation has to take place. This allows the more important projects and programmes to access the required resource and to move forward in accordance with their plans. Projects and programmes that are deemed low priority may have to revise their plans to take account of the reduced level of resources they potentially might receive, and those that no longer support the portfolio may need to be terminated.

Project and programme management have an important role to play in ensuring that portfolio management is provided with accurate up-to-date information, particularly on status. Project and programme managers may also have a significant role in influencing the portfolio prioritisation process, vying for the resources their project or programme may need at various stages of their life cycles.

APM Sample Paper

Question 58

Chapter 4 - Project life cycles

Assessment Criteria - assessment will require a learner to demonstrate that they can:

2.1 define the term project life cycle

2.2 state the phases of a typical project life cycle

2.3 identify reasons for structuring projects into phases

4.1 Project life cycles

A life cycle defines the inter-related phases of project, programme or portfolio and provides a structure for governing the progression of the work. (BoK 6)

Projects will always have a beginning and an end as do the phases within the cycle. How these are defined will vary depending on the type of project. The linear project life cycle or waterfall method follows as a generic sequence:

- **Concept.**
- **Definition.**
- **Development.**
- **Handover and closure.**

The extended project life cycle includes a further stage - **Benefits realisation**.

Concept

This establishes the need, problem or opportunity for the project. Often there will have been a prior report or feasibility study which may well have been run as an individual project.

The study will define the problem, it may have investigated what the real requirements are and it will have evaluated alternative solutions and recommended a course of action. This is transformed into the outline business case - often written by the project or programme manager with specialist support and to be approved by the project sponsor. If the preferred solution is supported at the gate review held at the end of this phase, the project continues to the definition phase.

Definition

This phase allows for further evaluation of the preferred solution and options to meet that solution. The Project Management Plan (PMP) together with a more detailed business case is delivered at the end of the phase to the project sponsor - the PMP is owned by the project manager.

Development

This phase implements the Project Management Plan. This phase may be divided into stages e.g. Design and Build:

Design

What is translated into how. The final deliverable takes shape through a process of user requirements, technical experts who create a solution to the problem expressed. This forms the blueprint for the build phase and comes in a variety of forms; diagrammatic plans, a working model, a prototype or a detailed specification.

Build

This is the phase where something tangible is created i.e. the tunnel dug, the building erected or the system built. This phase is always awaited with most impatience. This can lead to the temptation to skimp on the preceding phases in order to be seen to be producing something! This is a temptation to be resisted.

Handover and closure

This phase delivers the project to the sponsor and the organisation. The project is now complete in terms of delivery of a capability that will allow benefits to be achieved. See part 4.2 for more details.

Extended project life cycle

Benefits realisation - the outputs are transformed into outcomes by change managers to enable the benefits to be realised. New ways of working have to be embedded in business-as-usual to ensure that benefits continue to be realised.

Why are life cycle phases so important?

They ensure that there is sufficient time and resource for concept and definition phases.

Gate reviews between the phases allow for review of the business case - are the benefits still going to be realised, should the project continue?

They ensure that estimates are at an appropriate level for that phase (see chapter 7).

All phases of the life cycle are important; no phase should be omitted but they may overlap.

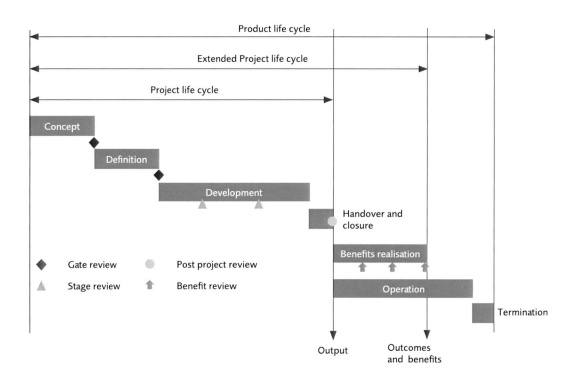

Fig. 2.1 Linear Project Lifecycle (BoK 6)

4.2 Handover and closure

Handover is that point in the life cycle where deliverables are handed over to the sponsor and users. Closure is the formal end point of a project or programme, either because it has been completed or because it has been terminated early. (BoK 6)

The **Handover** process may include:

- preparing the project deliverables for acceptance by the sponsor and the users;
- commissioning - this involves carrying out specified performance tests and operational trials to prove to the sponsor that acceptance criteria are being met;

- snagging - making any adjustments or modifications due to problems thrown up before or during commissioning;
- special training or familiarisation sessions with the sponsor's staff;
- ensuring that all project documentation is completed - to include any certificates, guarantees, warranties, operating instructions, maintenance manuals, quality control records and audit trails;
- acceptance by the sponsor of all relevant documentation;
- acceptance Certificate signed by the Sponsor to confirm acceptance;
- formal transfer of ownership and responsibility for the deliverables to the Sponsor - this may include taking on responsibility for insurance, maintenance etc.

The **Closure** process may include:

- phased closure based on tasks in the Work Breakdown Structure (see Chapter 6);
- demobilising or redeploying staff and disposing of any surplus materials and facilities;
- closing the accounts of the project;
- performance evaluations of team members are made together with any recommendations for staff development training;
- rewarding and recognising performance of team members;
- all project documentation and records are completed and archived;
- post-project review is undertaken to ensure that any lessons are learned;
- notice of closure should be sent to other staff within the organisation to inform them that no further activities are to be carried out or charges made.

APM Sample Paper

Questions - 27, 43, 57

Chapter 5 - What the project is

Assessment Criteria - assessment will require a learner to demonstrate that they can:

4.11 define success criteria in the context of managing projects

4.8 define the use of key performance indicators (KPIs)

4.12 define typical success factors that may contribute to successful projects

5.1 Project success criteria

Project success is the satisfaction of stakeholder needs and is measured by the success criteria as identified and agreed at the start of the project. (BoK 5)

Success criteria are the qualitative or quantitative measures by which the success of the project is judged. (BoK 6)

At handover and closure, it will be known whether a project has achieved its success criteria. As benefits may not be realised until after handover and closure, the ownership of benefits realisation rests with the sponsor rather than with the project manager.

The sponsor may view success as the project having achieved stated benefits as defined in the business case. From the project manager's perspective success may mean meeting agreed scope, time, cost and quality objectives as defined in the project management plan. Also, stakeholders may have differing views of the project's success which must be taken into account.

It is possible to have a successful project that fails to deliver expected benefits (e.g. the Millenium Dome (built on schedule and within the budget) and the Millennium Experience, a major exhibition contained within the Dome celebrating the beginning of the third millennium, which failed to attract the number of visitors anticipated) or a project that delivers significant benefits but is considered a failure. Therefore project success and benefits need to be considered together because it is the organisational impact of deliverables that produces benefits.

The Reports from the National Audit Office often make interesting reading. The report on shared service centres for government dated 7 March 2012 describes how central government spent seven years implementing shared services.

"The five centres we have examined cost £0.9 billion to build and operate core back-office functions. To date they have cost £1.4 billion, an overspend of £0.5 billion.

17

Departments have not realised the planned benefits. From the five centres we have examined the Government should, by its own estimates, have saved £159 million to the end of 2010-11. Only one can demonstrate a break-even on its investment. The two Centres still tracking benefits report a net cost of £235 Million."

Tracking benefits has not been a priority. Yet, the proposed benefits are the reason for carrying out projects and are clearly laid out in the business case.

For the project manager to understand what success is, **success criteria** must be agreed with stakeholders during the concept phase but may be changed at any time in the project's life cycle via change control. They include the main objectives of cost, quality and duration but go beyond them e.g. no reportable accidents. Success criteria require quantitative measures against which to judge whether success has been achieved.

5.2 **Key performance indicators** (KPIs)

KPIs are derived from success criteria. Key Performance Indicators are quantifiable measurements, agreed at the start of the project, that reflect the success criteria of the project.

It is important to keep the number of Key Performance Indicators small just to keep everyone's attention focused on achieving the same KPIs.

Key performance indicators should preferably meet the following essential criteria:

- be direct (no complex calculations);
- be objective;
- be quantitative;
- be practical;
- be reliable.

Tracking KPIs ensure that the project is progressing towards achievement of success criteria enabling corrective action to be taken. Examples of success criteria are:

- achievement of deliverables on time;
- recruitment of skilled resources.

5.3 Success Factors

Success factors used to be defined as "factors that when present in the environment are most conducive to the achievement of a successful project" (BoK5). Thus good weather was important in constructing the foundations of a building and meeting the deadlines.

In BoK 6 the definition has been refined to "management practices that, when implemented, will increase the liklihood of success of a project, programme or portfolio. The degree to which these practices are established and embedded within an organisation indicates its level of maturity."

So the presence of these practices does not guarantee project success, but their absence is likely to lead to project failure.

Examples of success factors include:

- defining clear goals and objectives,
- focusing on benefits arising from use of the project output,
- ensuring senior management commitment to the project.

APM Sample Paper

Questions - 8, 9, 38

Chapter 6 - Benefits - why the project should go ahead

Assessment Criteria - assessment will require a learner to demonstrate that they can:

4.7 define benefits management

6.1 Benefits

A benefit is *"the quantifiable and meaasurable improvement resulting from completion of the deliverables that is perceived as positive by a stakeholder. It will normally have a tangible value, expressed in monetary terms that will justify the investment. (BoK 6)*

"I didn't bid for the Olympics because I wanted three weeks of sport," London's mayor told an election hustings. *"I bid for the Olympics because it's the only way to get the billions of pounds out of the Government to develop the East End - to clean the soil, put in the infrastructure and build the housing."* Ken Livingstone as reported in Evening Standard 24th April 2008 - a clear indication of the importance he attached to the legacy.

Benefits are the main reason for carrying out projects. Chapter 7 will describe how benefits are included in the business case to enable a cost/benefit analysis which includes the uncertainties in the benefits and costs (risks). Firstly benefits must be discussed in more detail and the process of benefits management defined. Examples of benefits include:

- financial (profit or cost-effectiveness);
- improved customer service - fewer complaints;
- develop / enhance customer relationship(s) e.g. Guardian membership;
- development of competitive advantage;
- develop presence in a new market;
- longer term strategic advantage (e.g. new technology development);
- social benefits;
- environmental ('green' issues);

- PR value;

- operating necessity (e.g. response to regulatory changes);

- improved operational procedures / processes;

- staff motivation / morale / improved industrial relations.

Note that achievement of benefits may involve negative benefits or dis-benefits. A change in organisational structure with restructuring, may require a number of departures of long-serving staff, and the consequent loss of knowledge. Both benefits and dis-benefits have to be managed.

6.2 Benefits management

Benefits management is the identification, definition, planning, tracking and realisation of business benefits. (BoK 6)

Benefits management involves five main steps:

- Define benefits management plan - includes policies for measurement of benefits, roles and responsibilities, priorities and key performance indicators (KPIs).

- Identify and structure the benefits - they depend on delivery of outputs and secondly achievement of outcomes. Each benefit should be documented in terms of priority, interdependencies, value, timescales and ownership.

- Plan benefits realisation - includes capturing current performance of an operation so that the incremental benefit can be calculated. Milestones and schedule for benefits realisation need to be planned.

- Implement change - benefits come from the changes implemented - may include attitudes and behaviour.

- Realise benefits - includes embedding change.

APM Sample Paper

Question - 54

Chapter 7 - Estimating costs and benefits for the core business case

Assessment Criteria - assessment will require a learner to demonstrate that they can:

4.9 - part - identify typical estimating methods (including comparative, parametric)

7.1 Estimating methods

The business case for the project is developed during the first or concept stage; its purpose is to persuade senior management to provide funding for the second phase of the project - the definition phase - and then to guide the project manager in writing the project management plan. The business case is approved by the sponsor, who is accountable for achieving the benefits; it may be written by the programme or project manager possibly with specialist support.

Some projects are contracted out by the host organisation. The host's business case is based around the benefits accruing from the project, whereas the contractor's business case is based around the profitability of delivering the project output.

Look at the business case from the point of view of the sponsor. Money is being invested in the project to provide benefits to the organisation. Is it worth investing the costs to achieve the proposed benefits? This is the most important question that the business case seeks to address.

The core business case requires estimates of cost and benefits together with the uncertainties in each e.g cost = £100,000 +/- £15,000, benefits = £250,000 +/- f50,000. The uncertainties are derived from a review of the risks - both positive and negative see chapter 9 for details.

So it is important to ensure that the estimates of costs, benefits and uncertainties are as realistic as possible. However one often does not have a detailed plan of the design of the outputs and thus can only use data derived from similar projects. Two methods are particularly helpful:

1. Top-down estimating - Comparative estimating

Comparative or analogous estimating uses historic data from similar projects to determine the most appropriate cost and time. The data are compared by scaling of size, complexity and type of technology employed to determine a more informed estimate of the project's budget and schedule parameters.

2. Parametric estimating

Parametric estimating uses defined parameters by which a project can be measured, for example the cost or time to build a single deliverable, with this figure then being multiplied depending on the number of such parameters required. Examples are cost per square metre which is combined with projected floor area to generate building costs.

7.2 HS2 Example

Take the following data and estimate the cost of the planned HS2 railway line from London to Birmingham and the north of England:

Railway Line	Cost of construction (£B)	Length (km)
HS1	6.2 (1)	108 (2)
HS2	?	540 (3)

Notes:

1. From National Audit Office (NAO) report 28/03/2012 on the completion and sale of HS1. Cost is excluding financing costs and is at 2010 prices. Cost including financing costs = £10.2 B.

2. Also from NAO report 28/03/2012.

3. From original estimates of total length. Phase 1 route is agreed, phase 2 route is still to be determined.

4. HS1 is the high-speed railway line from the Channel Tunnel to London.

Estimated cost of HS2 = 6.2 x 540/108 = **£31.0 B**

This compares with the figures on the HS2 website on 6th February 2014 - estimated total costs of £42.6 B made up of Construction (**£28.2 B**) and Contingency (£14.4 B). It is very unusual to see such a large contingency (greater than 50%).

For a better comparison, allowance should be made for inflation from 2010 (HS1 actual figures) to 2011 (HS2 estimates).

We have, with minimal data, made a sensible estimate of the total project construction cost.

Interestingly the Project Assessment Review from the Cabinet Office on HS2 (relating to a review conducted in June 2012 but only released in June 2015) notes that the official estimates exclude:

- Escalation/inflation costs (figures are at Q2 2011 prices)
- Rolling stock costs (estimated at approximately £3 billion for phase 1 –and a further £5 billion for phase 2)
- DfT (Department for Transport) sponsor costs (and their advisers)
- TOC (train operating company) operator costs
- VAT
- Stamp duty on land purchase
- Exceptional hardship scheme (blight) costs
- Costs of over-site development
- Project costs accrued prior to 10 January 2012.

The Report recommended that a comprehensive budget for phase 1 of the project be drawn up, including all items currently excluded. This illustrates the additional work required to develop the initial estimates into an upgraded business plan presented and reviewed at the end of the second phase of the project life cycle - see Chapter 10.

APM Sample Paper

Question - 39

Chapter 8 - Environment and stakeholders

Assessment Criteria - assessment will require a learner to demonstrate that they can:

1.8 define the term project environment

1.9 define the components of the PESTLE acronym

4.6 define stakeholders and stakeholder management and explain why stakeholder management is important

8.1 Project context

The project context is defined as *"a collective term for the governance and setting of a project." (BoK 6)*

The setting is defined as *"the relationship of the project, programme or portfolio with its host organisation." (BoK6)*

Thus both context and setting are to do with the internal environment for the project.

Projects are managed according to a wide range of factors including the industry or business sector (e.g. IT or construction) in which it is based, geographical location, use of virtual teams, technical complexity or financial impact.

The following are examples of setting:

- procurement practices, such as the various standard forms of construction contract or the application of partnering, can shape organisational structures and ways of working;

- project management in drug development or the nuclear sector is strongly shaped by the regulatory requirements of licensing approval processes as well as by the scientific culture of the industry;

- projects within the UK government sector have to follow particular practices such as OGC Gateway (The Office of Government Commerce (OGC) examines a programme or project at critical points in its life cycle to provide assurance that it can progress successfully to the next phase). The OGC was an office of HM Treasury. However, following the credit crunch in 2007, it was absorbed into the Efficiency and Reform Group (ERG) within the Cabinet Office in May 2010. The OGC gateway review process still provides one of the best and most comprehensive sets of guidance for public projects;

- the use of publicly available methods such as PRINCE2 can have a huge effect on practice.

Variations in setting make the application of appropriate project management practices challenging. Their appropriateness will vary according to the variables described above.

All the above affect the context of the project and shape the environment that the sponsor, project manager and project team have to deal with, and may assist or restrict the attainment of the objectives, deliverable and benefits of the project. The successful accomplishment of a project generally requires a significant sensitivity to and understanding of both the internal and external environment in which it is based.

8.2 PESTLE analysis

The project external environment is outside the host organisation; its major elements are often described using the acronym PESTLE (**P**olitical, **E**conomic, **S**ociological, **T**echnical, **L**egal and **E**nvironment).

This is a tool to find out the current status and position of an organisation or individual in relation to their external environment and current role. The results can then be used as a basis for future planning and strategic management.

Depending on which elements are included it can also be referred to as STEP, STEEP, PESTEL or LEPEST. Recently it was even further extended to STEEPLE and STEEPLED, including education and demographics.

Depending on the scope and scale of the exercise being undertaken, you may want to consider for each factor:

- Which of the below are of most importance now?
- Which are likely to be most important in a few years?
- What are the factors influencing any changes?

Factor	Likely to include
Political What are the key political drivers of relevance?	What is happening politically in the environment in which you operate, including areas such as tax policy, employment laws, environmental regulations, trade restrictions and reform, tariffs and political stability. Context may include consideration of Worldwide, European and Government directives, funding council policies, national and local organisations' requirements, institutional policy.
Economic What are the important economic factors?	What is happening within the economy, for example; economic growth/ decline, interest rates, exchange rates and inflation rate, wage rates, minimum wage, working hours, unemployment (local and national), credit availability, cost of living, etc. Context may include consideration of funding mechanisms and streams, business and enterprise directives, internal funding models, budgetary restrictions, income generation targets.
Social What are the main societal and cultural aspects?	What is occurring socially in the markets in which you operate or expect to operate, cultural norms and expectations, health consciousness, population growth rate, age distribution, career attitudes, emphasis on safety, global warming. Context may include consideration of societal attitudes to education, particularly in relation to government directives and employment opportunities. Also general lifestyle changes, changes in populations, distributions and demographics and the impact of different mixes of cultures.
Technological What are current technology imperatives, changes and innovations?	What aspects of technological change may impact what you do? How will this impact your products or services; things that were not possible five years ago are now mainstream, for example mobile phone technology, blogs, social networking websites. New technologies are continually being developed and the rate of change itself is increasing. There are also changes to barriers to entry in given markets, and changes to financial decisions like outsourcing and insourcing.

Legal Current and impending legislation	What is happening with changes to legislation. This may impact employment, access to materials, quotas, resources, imports/ exports, taxation etc. Context may include European and national proposed and current legislation.
Environmental What are the environmental considerations , locally and further afield?	What is happening with respect to ecological and environmental aspects. Many of these factors will be economic or social in nature. Context may include local, national and international environmental impacts, outcomes of political and social factors.

You will tend to find a lot of crossover - for example policies under political factors leading to legal and environmental factors. You do not need to worry too much about pigeon-holing issues into the right category - the framework simply helps you think about the context as a whole.

8.3 Stakeholder management

Stakeholder management is the systematic identification, analysis, planning and implementation of actions designed to engage with stakeholders. (BoK 6)

Stakeholders are individuals or groups with an interest in the project, programme or portfolio because they are involved in the work or affected by the outcomes. (BoK 6)

Examples of stakeholders:

- Stakeholders can be both internal and external to the organisation.
- Interested parties from the wider environment e.g. government, press, focus groups, regulatory bodies.
- Those directly involved e.g. clients, users, providers of resources (human, material, financial).
- Those affected by the project but are not directly involved e.g. local community, competitors.
- Senior management who authorise resources needed for the project.

Stakeholder management is an iterative process which starts during the project concept phase.

Stakeholder identification requires consideration of who is involved in, affected by or can affect the project. Brainstorming of potential stakeholders may identify:

- Resources needed for the project
- Organisations or people who will be affected by the project
- Organisations or people on the sidelines of the project who will influence attitudes and Behaviours
- Statutory and regulatory bodies

Once stakeholders have been identified, **stakeholder analysis** is used to establish their position in relation to the project.

Questions to consider are as follows:

- How will they be affected by the project?
- Do they have a interest in the project succeeding?
- Will they be openly supportive of the project as it progresses?
- Is the stakeholder ambivalent about the project?
- Could the stakeholder have a negative view about what the project will deliver?
- What are their expectations and how can these be managed?
- Who and/or what might influence the stakeholder's views?

A tool to further understand a stakeholder's position in relationship to the project is a stakeholder grid. This is illustrated below:

	Against Project	Against Project	For Project	For Project
	High Interest	Low Interest	Low Interest	High Interest
High Influence/Power				
Low Influence/Power				

Use of stakeholder grid (Power/Interest matrix)

Rate each stakeholder or stakeholder group on a scale of 1 to 10 for both power to impact the project and extent of interest in the project (where 1 is very low and 10 is very high). Power is the ability to cause change to the project; interest is the probability that the power or influence is exerted.

Plot them on the above matrix.

Develop and agree a **stakeholder management/communication plan** according to their position on the matrix.

Considering a stakeholder's placement on this grid will help to determine stakeholder management actions. The stakeholder analysis will need to be validated against the project context as it often provides a good pointer towards how organisations and people will relate to the project outcomes. Stakeholders must be managed to ensure that their positive interest in the project is utilised and maintained or that their negative interest is removed or minimised. Stakeholders who are "for" the project and in a position of high power can be used to influence stakeholders who are "against" the project.

Stakeholder management becomes more complex when stakeholders' views are not consistent throughout the life cycle of the project as changes occur in their opinion, roles, views regarding the project and allegiances. The stakeholder analysis will need to be reviewed throughout the project life cycle.

The project's communication plan should be employed as a tool for stakeholder management. It may include who the stakeholders are and their communication needs, and who is responsible for their management and planned responses.

APM Sample Paper

Questions - 28, 40

Chapter 9 - Uncertainties in benefits and costs - risks

Assessment Criteria - assessment will require a learner to demonstrate that they can:

7.1 define risk

7.2 define risk management

7.3 explain the purpose of risk management

7.4 outline a high-level risk management process

7.5 describe the use of a risk register

9.1 Risk

There are two definitions for risk in the APM's Project Risk Analysis and Management (PRAM) Guide 2nd Edition (2004):

A. Risk Event:

This is an individual uncertainty and is defined as an uncertain event or set of circumstances that, should it occur, will have an effect on the achievement of the project's objectives.

B. Project Risk:

This is the overall joint effect of the individual risks and other sources of uncertainty. It is defined as the exposure of stakeholders to the consequences of variations in outcome.

All projects are unique which means they are likely to be subject to some risk. Even if this is just the uncertainty of the plan being based on estimates. The size and type of risk is dependent on the type of project.

The APM uses the term 'uncertainty' rather than 'risk' and identifies threats as well as opportunities. They also state that both can be managed through a single risk management process; this provides the option to take advantage of positive risks or opportunities.

9.2 Project Risk Management

Risk management is a process that allows individual risk events and overall risk to be understood and managed proactively, optimising success by minimising threats and maximising opportunities. (BoK 6)

Note that the updated 3rd edition (2011) of the book, Project Risk Management, by Chris Chapman and Stephen Ward has been retitled as "How to manage Project Opportunity and Risk - why uncertainty management can be a much better approach than risk management." This is reflected in the BoK 6 definition (above) of risk management - the emphasis on opportunity as well as threats, which may be linked by a common uncertainty.

The purpose of carrying out risk management is to optimise success (to achieve the best results possible in the project situation). This is done by minimising the negative uncertainties (threats) and maximising the positive uncertainties (opportunities).

The benefits of a systematic risk management process

- Informed planning: identifying risks informs the planning process and gives schedules, budget etc more credibility.
- Attainable business goals and project objectives: plans are therefore practical and realistic which improves the likelihood of achieving goals and objectives.
- Project viability: risk assessment allows for objective comparison of alternative approaches and assessment of project viability.
- Improve analysis and project planning: the use of a common risk assessment framework can provide valuable information that allows the collection of statistics and data that assists in planning future projects.
- Optimum risk ownership: risk management can properly and objectively assess who is best placed to manage risk and avoid 'buck passing'.

9.3 The Risk Management Process

The APM Project Risk and Management Guide second edition (2004) illustrates a generic risk management process.

It contains five phases together with a 'Manage Process' activity. This process is followed throughout the project.

The phases are:

- **Initiate** - defines project scope and objectives, environment and success criteria understood, agreement is reached on the risk management process that will apply to the project.

- **Identify** - determine and list the risks in the risk register.

- **Assess** - look at the structure of risks and their ownership, estimate the probability of occurrence and impact, and evaluate the severity of the risks. The relative significance of identified risks is assessed using qualitative techniques to enable them to be prioritised for further attention. Quantitative risk analysis may also be used to determine the combined effect of risk on overall project outcome. The range of techniques include the Monte Carlo simulation, decision trees and influence diagrams.

- **Plan responses** - this aims to avoid, reduce, transfer or accept threats as well as to exploit, enhance, share or accept opportunities with contingency for risks which cannot be handled proactively. Contingencies can include time, cost, resources and course of action.

- **Implement responses** - this is the implementation of agreed responses. This is invariably followed by iterative identification, review and update throughout the project life cycle to maintain awareness of current risk exposure. Therefore, the risk management process is an ongoing activity throughout the project, with assumptions and outcomes being reviewed as the project progresses.

Risk management begins at the concept phase of the project life cycle, in order to identify general risks and opportunities whilst making the business case in order to facilitate decision making in respect of project feasibility.

This rudimentary assessment will subsequently form the basis of a more in depth assessment that comes with the formal risk management process.

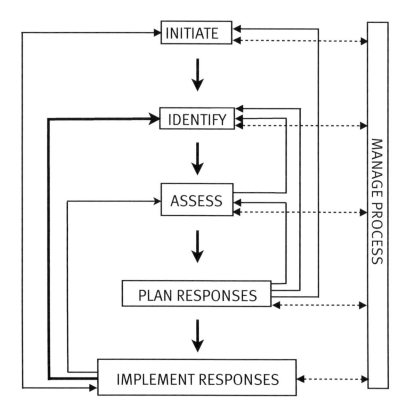

Figure 3.3 Phases of the risk management process (PRAM Guide 2nd edition 2004)

Note the bold feedback line from 'Implement responses' to 'Identify' - a major iterative loop.

9.4 The Risk Management Plan

A risk management plan should include the following:

- description of the project, its objectives and success criteria;
- the risk management process to be used (e.g. stages in the process; tools and techniques / software packages to be used; documentation; risk reviews and reporting procedures etc.);
- the criteria for the acceptability and tolerability of risk (to be used in the risk evaluation stage). This will reflect the attitude to risk of the organisations involved (e.g. what constitutes "excessive" risk);
- risk management organisation – identification of those involved in the process, their roles and responsibilities;

- internal and external interfaces between those involved in the risk management process;

- risk register (risk log);

- reference to applicable documents (e.g. company policies, project quality plan, contractor risk management plans etc.).

The risk management plan should be reviewed regularly and updated as required.

A key technique in qualitative assessment is the Probability–Impact (P-I) matrix also called a Likelihood–Consequence matrix.

The matrix is used to assess the relative importance and ranking of risks according to:

- the probability (likelihood) of the risk occurring;

- the severity of the impact (consequences) on the project.

The P-I matrix uses assigned numbers to categorise risks and provide an overall measure of their severity. These numbers are weighting factors and are not based on mathematical or statistical models – and are, therefore, qualitative (subjective) in nature.

Example: Meteorological Office - Weather warnings guide

The Office warns of severe or hazardous weather which has the potential to cause damage, widespread disruption and/or danger to life through the National Severe Weather Warning Service. This includes warnings about rain, snow, wind fog and ice.

Both likelihood and impact for a weather event are allocated a level on a 1 to 4 scale:

High - Medium - Low - Very Low

A tick can then be placed in the matrix representing that particular weather hazard.

These warnings are given a colour (red, amber or yellow) depending on a combination of both the likelihood of the event happening and the impact the conditions may have.

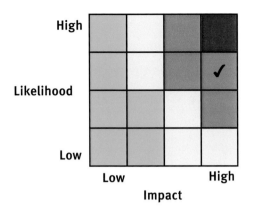

What the colours mean:

Yellow: Be aware. Severe weather is possible over the next few days and could affect you. Yellow means that you should plan ahead thinking about possible travel delays, or the disruption of your day to day activities. The Met Office is monitoring the developing weather situation and Yellow means keep an eye on the latest forecast and be aware that the weather may change or worsen, leading to disruption of your plans in the next few days.

Amber: Be prepared. There is an increased likelihood of bad weather affecting you, which could potentially disrupt your plans and possibly cause travel delays, road and rail closures, interruption to power and the potential risk to life and property. Amber means you need to be prepared to change your plans and protect you, your family and community from the impacts of the severe weather based on the forecast from the Met Office

Red: Take action. Extreme weather is expected. Red means you should take action now to keep yourself and others safe from the impact of the weather. Widespread damage, travel and power disruption and risk to life is likely. You must avoid dangerous areas and follow the advice of the emergency services and local authorities.

It can be seen from the figure that the colours are not distributed symmetrically. This is to weight the analysis towards the impact on the project, and thus emphasise the significance of low probability / high impact risk.

A contingency (e.g. extra budget, float in the project schedule to cover the necessary actions to get back on track) may be needed in any of the above strategies.

9.5 The Risk Register

The Risk Register (sometimes called a Risk Log) is a key output of the risk management process, and a key document in the management of risk.

The Risk Register provides a summary of all the risks and their current status; it is a living document that is continually updated and reviewed.

The compilation of the Risk Register commences at the very beginning of the risk management process. A significant early version of this will be prepared at the Definition stage.

It is the means by which risk status is recorded and reported and should contain the following information:

- A list of identified risks and a description of each (the nature of each risk).
- Project phase of impact (When).
- Probability / impact assessment.
- The consequences of the risk on the project (time, cost, performance, safety, liability, security etc.).
- The owner of each risk (the individual responsible for managing the risk).
- Summary of treatment action(s).
- Timescale and cost of treatment.
- Current ranking of each risk.

APM Sample Paper

Questions - 3, 19, 33, 42, 49

Chapter 10 - Full business case and project management plan

Assessment Criteria - assessment will require a learner to demonstrate that they can:

4.4 identify the purpose and the typical content of a business case

4.5 define the role of the sponsor and project manager in relation to the business case

4.1 state the main purpose of a project management plan

4.2 define who is involved in the creation of the project management plan

4.3 explain why the project management plan needs to be approved, owned and shared

10.1 Business case

The business case provides justification for undertaking a project or programme. It evaluates the benefit, cost and risk of alternative options and provides a rationale for the preferred solution. (BoK 6)

The contents of the full business case go beyond the core business case and will include (BoK 6):

- strategic case - alignment with the organisation's strategy;
- options appraisal - includes investment appraisal of the options;
- expected net benefits after any negative benefits are taken into account;
- commercial aspects - costs - includes financing costs based on cash flow calculations;
- risk - the uncertainties in primarily the costs and benefits;
- timescales - a summary of the delivery of outputs and realisation of benefits.

In practice, the contents do vary depending on the type of project. For example projects which require a careful handling of health and safety issues, such as railways or nuclear power, will devote a section to explaining how adherence to the appropriate safety standards will be achieved.

The outputs that are required to enable the benefits to be achieved need to be specified to enable costs to be calculated. For HS2 this might be the length of track - 540 km (perhaps also the proportion in a tunnel) - and the number of stations - see chapter 5 on estimating HS2 costs.

The full business case for the project is developed during the first or concept stage; its primary purpose is to persuade senior management to provide funding for the second phase of the project - the definition phase. It is approved by the sponsor, who is accountable for achieving the benefits. The case may be written by the programme or project manager possibly with specialist support.

Some projects are contracted out by the host organisation. The host's business case is based around the benefits accruing from the project, whereas the contractor's business case is based around the profitability of delivering the project output.

It is then reviewed and developed in detail for inclusion in the Project Management Plan during the second phase. Often senior management may indicate to the sponsor that further work is needed to clarify the proposed benefits of the project. Additional marketing research may be carried out to re-evaluate the accuracy of suggested revenue projections. Note that there is a tendency for project proposers to overestimate the benefits and underestimate the costs - optimism bias.

During the development or third phase of the project, the business case is reviewed regularly to ensure that the planned benefits are still capable of being achieved.

The business case requires a 'businesslike' approach - meaning systematic or practical. Thus this approach is necessary for all requests for funding, including those to the Heritage Lottery Fund.

10.2 Project Management Plan

The project management plan brings together all the plans for a project. The purpose of the project management plan (PMP) is to document the outcomes of the planning process and to provide the reference document for managing the project. The project management plan is owned by the project manager. (BoK 5)

The Project Management Plan (PMP) is the output of the definition phase of a project or programme. (BoK 6)

Planning is an iterative process that goes on throughout the life of your project. The plan is a living thing that isn't finished until the project is complete. Developing the initial plan is usually a very optimistic stage in the project, especially in the public sector. Though this is considered work in progress, once you have a plan you can measure progress against it and re-plan as necessary. Ad hoc or inadequate approaches to planning are quite stressful so it pays to plan in a methodical manner. Planning is important but so is having a built in level of flexibility which allow the planning and review to continue throughout the project. The plan helps you understand where you are and puts you in control.

The project management plan is also referred to as a project execution plan, a project implementation plan, a project plan or a plan. In the PRINCE2 methodology, the equivalent to the PMP is called the project initiation document (PID). This also brings together all the plans in one document allowing formal project authorisation to proceed to phase three.

The project management plan confirms the agreements between the sponsor, other stakeholders and the project manager. It is approved by the sponsor, representing the organisation, with the project manager, representing the project team. Sharing the PMP with stakeholders is important in establishing common agreement of the contents, especially as the stakeholders' expectation of the project may have changed during the planning process. Although the project manager owns the PMP it should be developed with the project team; this removes ambiguity, develops commitment and assists in effective handover of the project.

The PMP documents how the project will be managed in terms of **why, what, how, who, when, where and how much**:

- The **why** is primarily about benefits that may be realised from the changes to be delivered using the outputs. This will include a definition of the need, problem or opportunity being addressed. This should be developed in the business case.

- The **what** describes the objectives, a description of the scope, the deliverables and their acceptance criteria. It also describes the success criteria for the project and the Key Performance Indicators (KPIs) that will be measured in order to achieve success. The what needs to take into account the project's constraints, assumptions and dependencies.

- The **how** defines the strategy for management, the handover of the project, the tools and techniques, monitoring and control and reporting arrangements.

- The **who** includes a description of the key project roles and responsibilities and the plan for all the resources that will be required.

- **When** defines the timescales, including milestones and any arrangements for phasing, which must also then be reflected in the **how much**.

- **Where** defines the geographical location(s) where the work is performed, which impacts on costs and personnel factors.

- **How much** defines the project budget and the budgeting and cost management process.

The 5 W's and 1 H (excluding How much) have often been used as an aid to information gathering, such as police reports, and journalism. They were referred to by Rudyard Kipling, who had been a journalist in India, in the Just So Stories - The Elephant's Child - "I keep six honest serving men (They taught me all I knew); Their names were What and Why and When and How and Where and Who".

The PMP also describes the policies and plans for managing changes, communication, configuration, governance, health safety and environment issues, procurement, quality and risk; many of these policies may be common to all projects within an organisation. The plans show how the policies will be implemented in the project.

The PMP is progressively developed during the planning process and is managed as a live, configuration-controlled document. In order to develop the PMP, scope management, scheduling, resource management and budgeting and cost management will be required. Once agreed, the PMP provides a **baseline** description of how the project will be managed, which is then periodically reviewed and updated through change control. The PMP will itself be the baseline document upon which changes are considered.

10.3 Use of PMP during project life cycle

Before the PMP is developed, the project strategy is developed by the project manager and agreed with the sponsor. The project strategy is used to determine approaches to be taken by the project e.g. outsourcing, priorities between time, cost and quality and the project team structure. Then the PMP is developed during the definition phase of the project.

Remember the PMP is a living document which should always represent an up-to-date view of the project. It is a controlled document therefore should not be subject to

44

ad hoc, unnecessary or unsanctioned changes. There should only be one version of the PMP in use.

Changes to the PMP will occur throughout the project life cycle. Changes to time, cost and performance are likely to occur as the design phase may highlight issues that have not yet been considered. The build phase is likely to highlight issues.

Contents of PMP

Contents of a PMP are project specific. In addition the nature and size of a project, the practices and culture of the organisation in question also have an impact on the PMP.

As plans tend to vary in format and content, a comprehensive template for a project management plan can be found in BS6079-1 (2010) Guide to Project Management.

The Project Management Plan generally includes the following:

Background information and success criteria

- Sponsor.
- Business Benefits.
- Project Objectives.
- Success Criteria.
- Key Performance Indicators.

Administrative details

- PMP Configuration Details.
- Contents List.
- List of Amendments - amendments to the document from one issue to the next, which should include summary of details, rationale for the change and date of incorporation.
- Applicable Documents - list of mandated policies and standards to which the project is obliged to conform, e.g. legal, organisation policies.

- Reference Documents - list of guidelines which should be referred to during the planning and execution of the project, e.g. project management, configuration management, quality control, non-conformance reporting, risk management, project organisation, systems management.
- Circulation and contacts list.
- List of Associated Contracts.

Specific Plans and Policies

- Risk Management Plan.
- Issue Management Plan.
- Health, Safety and Environment Management Plan.
- Communications Plan.
- Stakeholder Management Plan.
- Document Distribution Plan.
- Quality Management Plan.

Configuration Management and Change Control.

These may be specific to the project, and/or refer to corporate policies, for example Quality or Environmental Management Systems.

Work Breakdown Structure (WBS)

A hierarchical breakdown of the work necessary to complete the project, structured in a way appropriate for its effective management. A project WBS directory can be included which gives task names, codes and brief summary. A dictionary of task definitions may also be included if the reader is likely to be unfamiliar with the terminology employed.

Schedule

The time plan for the work to be done - an overall schedule of the work necessary to complete the project usually presented as a Gantt chart (and possibly also network). A list of project milestones should be included which briefly describes each milestone and their delivery date. A list of all deliverables by time and responsible owner will provide focus for the project team.

Commitment Acceptance

Once the division of responsibilities within the project has been identified, commitment from the task owners to discharge these responsibilities (and any caveats) should be recorded in the PMP. As work progresses, instructions to proceed and budget releases should be recorded in the budget log.

APM Sample Paper

Questions - 10, 11, 25, 41, 55

Chapter 11 - Quality management

Assessment Criteria - assessment will require a learner to demonstrate that they can:

8.1 define quality

8.2 define quality management

8.3 define the following: quality planning, quality assurance, quality control and continual improvement

8.4 outline the difference between quality control and quality assurance

11.1 Quality

Quality is defined in the BoK6 glossary as " *The fitness for purpose or the degree of conformance of the outputs of a process or the process itself*".

Quality is a complex and multi-faceted topic. David Garvin in his book on "Managing Quality", summarized five principal approaches to defining quality:

- **Transcendental View of Quality**: Those who hold a transcendental view would say, "I can't define it, but I know when I see it."

- **Product-Based View**: Product based definitions are different. Quality is viewed as quantifiable and measurable characteristics or attributes. For example durability or reliability can be measured (e.g. mean time between failure, fit and finish), and the engineer can design to that benchmark. Quality is determined objectively.

- **User-Based View**: User based definitions are based on the idea that quality is an individual matter, and products that best satisfy their preferences (i.e. perceived quality) are those with the highest quality.

- **Manufacturing-Based View**: Manufacturing-based definitions are concerned primarily with engineering and manufacturing practices and use the universal definition of "conformance to requirements." Requirements, or specifications, are established design, and any deviation implies a reduction in quality. The concept applies to services as well as products. Excellence in quality is not necessarily in the eye of the beholder but rather in the standards set by the organization.

- **Value-Based View**: Value-based quality is defined in terms of costs and prices as well as a number of other attributes. Thus, the consumer's purchase decision is based on quality (however it is defined) at the acceptable price.

The APM definition is based on the user-viewpoint - fitness for purpose - and the manufacturing viewpoint - conformance to requirements or specification; the two most relevant to project management.

11.2 Quality management

Quality management is a discipline for ensuring that both the outputs, benefits, and the processes by which they are delivered, meet the required needs of the stakeholders requirements and are fit for purpose. (BoK 6)

It involves all management activities and functions involved in determination of quality policy and its implementation through means such as quality planning, quality assurance, quality control and continual improvement.

11.3 Quality Processes

- Quality planning.
- Quality assurance.
- Quality control.
- Continuous improvement.

The requirements for quality, expressed in measurable terms are acceptance criteria; they form the foundation for quality management for the project.

Quality planning - the requirements for quality are identified; then the project manager prepares to achieve those requirements by checking and recording the actions needed to achieve the standard set out by the requirements. The project manager then is able to manage the trade off between scope, time, cost and quality. Outputs and process can only be fit for purpose if the purpose is understood.

So the Quality Plan in the PMP outlines out how quality will be achieved for both the project management processes and for the product. It is normal for these to be in line with organisational norms for quality.

There are standards from the International Organization for Standardization of particular relevance:

- ISO 9000:2005 Quality management systems — Fundamentals and vocabulary; it deals with the fundamentals of quality management systems, including the eight management principles on which the family of standards is based.
- ISO 9001:2008 deals with the requirements that organisations wishing to meet the standard have to fulfill (an updated version is expected at the end of 2015).
- ISO 9004:2009 Managing for the sustained success of an organisation; A quality management approach.

Quality management systems require documentation in the form of a quality manual which includes the quality policy, system, objectives, procedures, detailed work processes and departmental responsibilities. It is the responsibility of the project manager to ensure that there is a quality system within his/her project and that this is compatible with the organisational approach to quality.

In addition, ISO 21500:2012, Guidance on project management, provides high-level description of concepts and processes that are considered to form good practice in project management. It is a high level standard designed to provide an overarching framework that facilitates the development of national standards, bodies of knowledge, competency frameworks and methodologies that align to a common set of principles and definitions so that the information is transferrable between organisations and countries.

Quality assurance provides confidence to stakeholders that requirements for quality will be achieved. Quality assurance validates the consistent use of procedures and standards, supported by independent reviews and quality audits. Quality assurance will also be a source of lessons learned and ideas for improvement.

Quality assurance aims to ensure the likelihood of achieving the desired quality the first time. This process can be seen as a measure that attempts to avoid poor quality.

Quality assurance involves:

- clarity - objective and requirements must be clear, comprehensive and coherent;
- implementing proven approaches - the application of standards;
- the use of qualified resources - both people and materials - qualified resource can be demonstrated to perform to the required standard i.e.
  - Professional accreditation of people.
  - Review of data/documentation associated with materials or components.
- Configuration management;
- Implementing an effective project life cycle which allows for phasing and design reviews.

Quality control - this is the process that ensures conformity to agreed standard by:

- Inspecting, testing and quality measurement - verifies that the project deliverables conform to specification, are fit for purpose and meet stakeholder expectations.
- This can be considered a curative process as it is designed to correct any deficiencies in quality that are found.

The success of Quality assurance and Quality control can be enhanced by using a number of tools and techniques including project risk management, modelling and testing and configuration management. Configuration management will support the effective control of documentation and physical items.

Concepts that further define quality are 'right first time' and 'zero defects' since rework costs the project time and money and reduces stakeholder confidence. Accepting outputs to a reduced specification may allow the project to meet requirements for time and cost, but is poor project quality management. Delivering results to a higher specification, sometimes called gold-plating is also poor quality.

Continuous improvement - this is partially a feedback mechanism from quality control and quality assurance into quality planning, but goes further.

Organisations that achieve project quality demonstrate a continual systematic approach to improvement, i.e. continuous improvement, that is focused on specifying requirements tightly and meeting them without wasting time or resources in the process. The practices encompassed in total quality management (TQM), sigma six and lean are designed to achieve results as efficiently and effectively as possible.

The drive for total quality has led to the development of maturity models designed to measure attainment and provide the motivation and a mechanism for objectively achieving improvement. Models such as the EFQM excellence model, the project excellence model, and a wide range of other capability maturity models also allow benchmarking between organisations and wider improvement across an organisation or sector.

11.4 Cost and Benefits of Quality

Quality incurs costs in two ways: Firstly, the cost of poor quality, for example:

- Internal failure, e.g. management time, scrapped materials; cost of rework.
- External failure, e.g. customer goodwill; warranty; litigation.

The second cost is in the processes and steps necessary to improve quality, such as:

- Prevention, e.g. process and product design improvements; proactive identification of potential problems; staff training and development.
- Appraisal, e.g. statistical testing, data processing, problem investigation.

The classical model of total quality costs (failure costs plus prevention & appraisal costs) is shown in the following diagram. As more is spent on prevention & appraisal the failure costs fall. The total costs drop to a minimum where the two lines cross and then increase again. This model indicates that one should aim at the minimum total quality costs.

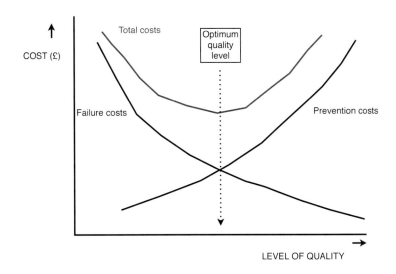

Figure 11.1 Total costs of quality - classical model

In many cases this model is flawed - it assumes constant sales. When one accepts the possibility of zero defects, the aim is to eliminate the causes of poor quality. Quality levels can be economically improved very close to perfection. Similarly the APM aim is that all projects are successful - zero failures.

The benefits of implementing quality management generally outweigh the investment:

- Cost savings (e.g. it can cost more to correct a problem in a process or a product than to prevent it in the first place).

- Customer satisfaction, better customer relations (e.g. leading to repeat business, enhanced industry reputation etc.).

- Accreditation of an organisation's Quality System to a quality standard (e.g. ISO series). This is a prerequisite for many sectors of business and industry (e.g. in many organisations, only suppliers with ISO 9000 accreditation are invited to respond to a tender).

APM Sample Paper

Questions - 2, 18, 32

Chapter 12 - Reviews

Assessment Criteria - assessment will require a learner to demonstrate that they can:

8.5 identify the purpose of:

- gate reviews
- post project reviews
- benefit reviews
- peer reviews
- project audits

12.1 Project reviews

A review is a critical evaluation of a deliverable, business case or P3 management process. (BoK 6)

Diagram 12.1 shows four of the different types of review:

- Project Evaluation review.
- Gate review.
- Post-Project review.
- Benefits Realisation review.

Project evaluation review

These reviews are undertaken by the Project Manager throughout the project life cycle - these meetings allow reflection by the project team on performance, primarily reviewing progress against the project management plan (PMP). They include the stage reviews in figure 12.1. The aims of the Project Evaluation Review are to:

- evaluate the project management processes used;
- establish any lessons learned and actions arising from them;
- raise any concerns and agree corrective actions;

- review the likely technical success of the project;

- validate overall progress against the plan - schedule, budget, resources, quality;

- review risks;

- consider stakeholder relationships and perceptions.

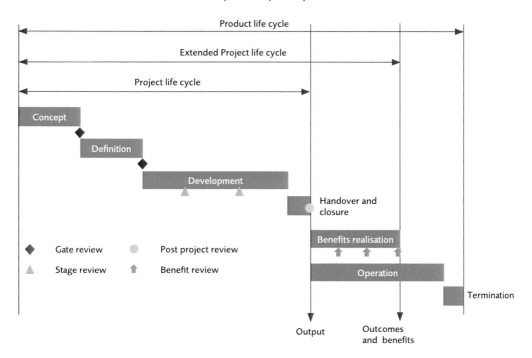

Figure 12.1 The project and extended life cycles (APM BoK 6th edition)

Gate review

These are undertaken at the end of a phase or stage of the project life cycle to determine whether the project should move into the next phase or stage. The sponsor is able to decide whether to authorise expenditure on the next stage.

The Gate Review considers:

- conclusions and supporting data from the most recent Project Evaluation Review;

- any deliverables completed during the phase or stage eg Business Plan at the end of the Concept Phase;

- plans for the next phase eg the Project Management Plan at the end of the Definition Phase;
- any changes in the external environment and thus changes in risk.

Post-Project review

This review takes place after handover of the deliverables but before closure of the project. The aims of the review are to:

- evaluate the project against its success criteria;
- determine what went right and what went wrong, distinguishing between causes and effects;
- recognise individual and team performance;
- evaluate the project management processes and any tools or techniques used;
- learn lessons that will allow the organisation to improve its processes for future projects.

Note that within Prince2 the Post-Project review has a different meaning - it is a review held after project closure to determine if the expected benefits have been obtained.

Benefits realisation review

This review is organised by the Project Sponsor and is held after the project closure and a following period of business-as-usual. It is designed to establish that the expected benefits have been obtained. As benefits may take several years to come to full fruition, several benefits reviews may be held.

Audits

In addition to these reviews organised by the project manager or sponsor, it may be thought necessary to open the project management process to external audit i.e. outside the project team. This may be by the organisation's internal audit or the project/programme office or by an external third-party organisation. This a formal process often with a list of points to be complied with.

Peer review

A peer review is not a "required" review but is requested by the person responsible for a task or work package. It is carried out by someone with the required skills or experience. An example would be a peer review of a Project Management Plan by another project manager to check that there are no errors or omissions.

APM Sample Paper

Questions - 31, 47

Chapter 13 - Scope management

Assessment Criteria - assessment will require a learner to demonstrate that they can:

5.1 define project scope management

5.2 describe how product breakdown structure (PBS) and work breakdown structure (WBS) are used to illustrate the scope of work required

5.3 define the uses of:

- Cost Breakdown Structure (CBS)

- Organisational Breakdown Structure (OBS)

- Responsibility Assignment Matrix (RAM)

13.1 Scope management

Scope is the totality of the outputs, outcomes and benefits and the work required to produce them. (BoK 6)

Scope management is the process whereby outputs, outcomes and benefits are identified, defined and controlled. (BoK 6)

Defining and managing the project scope influences the project's overall success. Each project requires a careful balance of tools, data sources, methodologies, processes and procedures, and other factors to ensure that the effort expended on scoping activities is commensurate with the project's size, complexity, and importance. For example, a critical project could merit formal, thorough, and time-intensive scoping activities, while a routine project could require substantially less documentation and scrutiny. The project management team documents these scope management decisions in the project scope management plan. The project scope management plan is a planning tool describing how the team will define the project scope, develop the detailed project scope statement, define and develop the work breakdown structure, verify the project scope, and control the project scope.

It is important to define what is outside of the scope, i.e. the deliverable the project will not provide. Scope management is continually applied through out the project life cycle.

A high level statement of scope is documented in the business case. This describes the breadth of the scope. The depth of the scope is described at differing levels of detail as the project progresses.

Scope management involves:

- Requirements management - gathers and assesses stakeholder needs and wants.
- Solutions development - works out how the requirements may be achieved.
- Benefits management - takes requirements expressed in terms of benefits and manages them through to delivery.
- Change management - deals with the transformation of business-as-usual in order to use the project outputs to achieve outcomes and realise benefits.
- Change control - control of requests to change the baseline scope of a project.
- Configuration management - monitors and documents the description of the deliverables.

13.2 Breakdown structures

The scoping of a project involves developing the following:

- **Product breakdown structure (PBS)** - identifies deliverables and breaks them into manageable elements.
- **Work breakdown structure (WBS)** - determines the work required to produce the deliverables of the product breakdown structure.

The product breakdown structure (PBS) defines all the products (deliverables) that the project will produce. The lowest level of a product breakdown structure is a product (deliverable). Therefore the product breakdown structure is a break down of items to be delivered not the tasks required to deliver them.

The product breakdown structure sub-divides each of the components to the lowest level item. It is normally at this point that purchasing specifications or manufacturing drawings are drawn up.

Older texts suggest that one way of preparing the PBS is to use sticky notes on a white board. This is still used but often it may be easier to use mind-mapping software, because the software can re-arrange the content as new entries are made. The mind map is a breakdown structure but laid out in a different way with the title in the middle of the diagram, rather than in its usual position at the top of the diagram.

The following diagram illustrates such an approach:

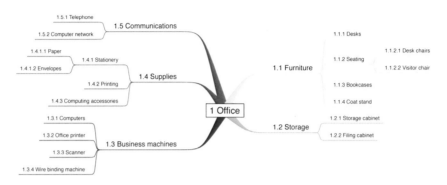

Figure 13.1 A mind map for the product breakdown structure.

Note that some mind-mapping software can feed data straight into project management software packages.

The software may show the mind map in an alternative way ie an indented list - this is one form of the Product Breakdown Structure:

1 Office

    1.1 Furniture

        1.1.1 Desks

        1.1.2 Seating

            1.1.2.1 Desk chairs

            1.1.2.2 Visitor chair

        1.1.3 Bookcases

        1.1.4 Coat stand

    1.2 Storage

        1.2.1 Storage cabinet

        1.2.2 Filing cabinet

1.3 Business machines

    1.3.1 Computers

    1.3.2 Office printer

    1.3.3 Scanner

    1.3.4 Wire binding machine

1.4 Supplies

    1.4.1 Stationery

        1.4.1.1 Paper

        1.4.1.2 Envelopes

    1.4.2 Printing

    1.4.3 Computing accessories

1.5 Communications

    1.5.1 Telephone

    1.5.2 Computer network

This is the basis for diagram 13.2 of the Product Breakdown Structure: In the diagram, only the furniture and supplies at level 2 are expanded in order to keep the diagram of manageable size - full details are in the indented list.

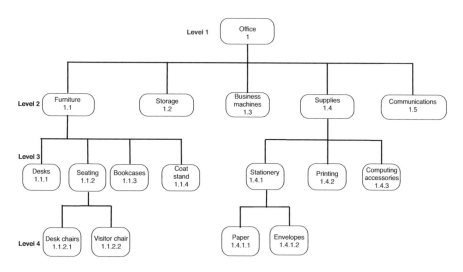

Figure 13.2 Diagram of the Product Breakdown Structure

The work breakdown structure (WBS) is the next stage and defines the work required to produce the deliverables in the PBS. The lowest level of detail normally shown in a work breakdown structure is the work package. Activities may not be shown on the work breakdown structure if this is considered to be too great a level of detail. Acceptance criteria for each work package must be established as part of the ongoing project quality management process.

Therefore the work breakdown structure:

- provides a complete picture of the project's scope of work;
- acts as a checklist to ensure areas of work / tasks are not missed or forgotten;
- provides a basis for identifying and assigning needed resources;
- enables the estimation and allocation of costs for the work (budget management);
- provides the basis for allocation of work responsibility to individuals;
- is the foundation for the project schedule;

The WBS sets out the work to be done as a hierarchy of activities – organised into work packages.

As with the PBS, the WBS may be presented as a numbered, hierarchical diagram or indented list.

Work breakdown structures can be organised using three approaches. The WBS must be organised using the approach that enables effective management of the project.

- **Product based**
- **Process based**
- **Organisation based**

Product-based. The organisation of the WBS is based around the PBS, but will also include activities that transcend all components.

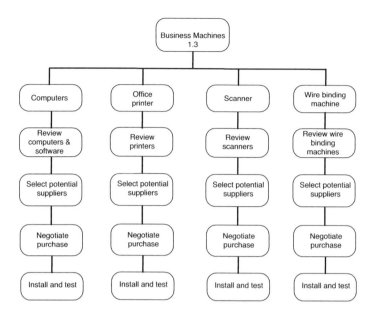

Figure 13.3 Product-Based Work Breakdown Structure

Process-based. The WBS is based around the type of work to be done. There are many variations on this theme. Some common ways of organising process-based WBS are by:

- Discipline (e.g. in a construction project : civil engineering, plumbing, electrical).
- Project life cycle phases (e.g. feasibility, definition, design, build etc.).
- Sub-project, where the project is broken down into a collection of sub-projects. This is useful where a main contractor is using many sub-contractors.

Organisation-based. The WBS is organised according to the project organisation, e.g. department, location, contractor, cost centre code.

The choice of approach will depend upon the nature of the project and the division of responsibilities within the co-operating organisations.

BS6079 notes that the product-based approach is often the most useful. This is true when the project involves clear physical deliverables and is extensively used in manufacturing.

A Process-Based WBS. An administrative project lends itself more to a work-based WBS design e.g.

o Market Research Project

1.0 Produce Brief

    1.1 Problem Definition

    1.2 Research Design

2.0 Questionnaire Design

3.0 Fieldwork

4.0 Data Processing

    4.1 Programme System

    4.2 Write Specification

        4.2.1 Select Input Data

        4.2.2 Select Output Data

            4.2.2.1 Specify Cross-Tabs

            4.2.2.2 Specify Format

    4.3 Pilot

5.0 Data Analysis

6.0 Project Management

Work Definition Sequence

Once the WBS has been determined, the project (time) schedule (network, Gantt, milestones) can be developed. The project schedule defines the interdependencies between the tasks in the WBS. The following diagram indicates the sequence of development of the Project Management Plan from the breakdown structures:

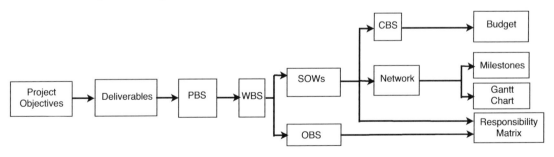

Figure 13.5 Development of the PMP

CBS = Cost Breakdown Structure - see the next chapter, Chapter 14

OBS = Organisational Breakdown structure - see Chapter 13

SoW = Statement of Work - not used in all industries.

APM Sample Paper

Questions - 6, 7, 22, 36, 37, 52, 60

Chapter 14 - Estimating

Assessment Criteria - assessment will require a learner to demonstrate that they can:

4.9 - part - identify typical estimating methods (including analytical)

4.10 describe the estimating funnel

14.1 Estimating and errors in estimating

Estimating uses a range of tools and techniques to produce estimates. An estimate is an approximation of project time and cost targets that is refined throughout the project life cycle. (BoK 5 - BoK 6 removes the second sentence.)

The original budget for the London 2012 Summer Olympics was £2.4 billion, but this was increased almost fourfold to about £9.28 billion in 2007. Actual costs were put at £8.77 billion in July 2013. What causes such inaccuracy in project estimates?

Causes of Estimating Errors

- Social and political factors - pressure from senior management or client.
- Lack of estimating experience.
- Poor understanding of what an estimate requires.
- Lack of input to the estimating process.
- Psychological factors - optimism or pessimism.

HM Treasury Green Book (April 2013) on Optimism Bias - *"Project appraisers have the tendency to be over optimistic. Explicit adjustments should therefore be made to the estimates of a project's costs, benefits and duration, which should be based on data from past or similar projects, and adjusted for the unique characteristics of the project in hand."*

People tend to under-estimate costs and over-estimate benefits.

Daniel Kahneman - Thinking, fast and slow (2011) - describes the problems associated with the two systems that drive the way we think and make choices. One system (1) is fast , intuitive and emotional, the other (2) is slower, more deliberative and more logical. He exposes faults associated with fast or system 1 thinking. Estimating has to be system 2 based to minimise these faults.

14.2 Estimates across the life-cycle

At the start of a project, estimates of cost have low accuracy. As the project proceeds, estimates are refined and become more accurate. This is sometimes illustrated using an estimation funnel showing the spread of estimates during a project (see figure 5.1 from BoK 6). A similar concept is the cone of uncertainty which describes the reduction in the amount of uncertainty during a project.

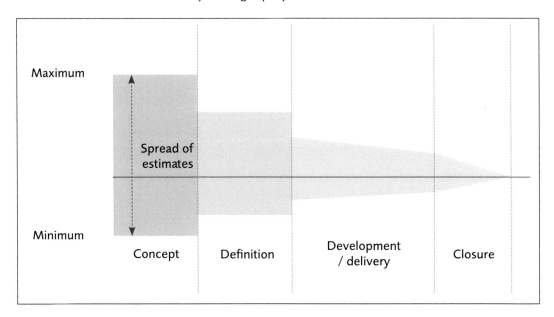

Figure 5.1 The Estimating Funnel (BoK 6) concerning costs

Note: In the light of our discussion on optimism this diagram does not make sense. If 'Spread of estimates' on the vertical axis is replaced by 'Estimating accuracy', the diagram then appears consistent. The uncertainty is mainly upwards, because people tend to underestimate costs,.

In chapter 7 we introduced parametric and comparative estimating to aid in developing estimates of cost and benefits for the business case. Now we describe methods that may be used in developing the PMP.

Bottom-up estimating -analytical estimating

The bottom-up method uses the work breakdown structure (described in the previous chapter - itemises the work required to produce the project deliverables) derived to a level of detail that allows estimates to be provided of cost and time for the project activities.

Three-point estimating

A three-point estimate is an estimate in which the most likely mid-range value (m), an optimistic value (a) and a pessimistic, worst-case value (b) are given. The PERT technique for estimating activity duration uses a weighted average to calculate the expected time for an activity.

Estimate = (a + 4m + b) / 6

Standard deviation, D = (b − a) / 6

i.e. Confidence level is about 68% that actual value lies within the range of plus or minus D or 95% within plus or minus 2D.

Example 1

Time to travel from home in Tunbridge Wells to Central London:

a = 80 minutes; b = 260 minutes ; m = 90 minutes.

Estimated time = 117 minutes.

For some applications, a different and simpler formula may be used - Estimate = (a + m + b) / 3

"The most important thing I've learned about good estimates is that they only come from credible designs and requirements. Good engineering estimates are possible only if you have two things: good information and good engineers."

Scott Berkun (2008) in his book on mastering project management - Making Things Happen.

APM Sample Paper

Questions - 24, 53

Chapter 15 - Time Scheduling

Assessment Criteria - assessment will require a learner to demonstrate that they can:

6.1 Identify the purpose of scheduling

6.2 outline different approaches to scheduling (including critical path analysis, total float, Gantt (bar) charts, baseline, milestone)

Schedule management is the process of developing, maintaining and communicating schedules for time and resource. (BoK 6)

15.1 Time scheduling

Time scheduling is a collection of techniques used to develop and present schedules that show when work will be performed. (BoK 6)

The project schedule:

- Provides the basis for resource planning – e.g. when specific skills might be needed.
- Leads to the development of the project's S-curve. The cumulative cost of resources (labour) over time i.e. the spend profile.
- Highlights critical activities and milestones.
- Plays a crucial role in the monitoring and management of project progress.

The project schedule is developed by the project manager during the second or Definition phase of the project life cycle. Project team members should be involved in the development of detailed schedules; this increases the likelihood that the project will contain realistic timeframes, and improves commitment if team members are involved rather than having timescales given to them.

The preparation of the project schedule contains the following key steps:

- Take activities as defined in the WBS.
- Estimate durations for each activity.

- Work out the dependencies for each activity.
- Develop the network & calculate the total duration of the project, its critical path and float.

Developing the schedule is an iterative process and the overall constraints of the project, for example resource constraints or absolute requirements with regard to time (e.g. constructing the Millennium Dome in time for its opening to the public on 1 January 2000) must be taken into consideration when scheduling. The final project schedule is agreed with the sponsor and is then baselined, to be used in the third phase to monitor progress, assess and agree any changes. Any changes which affect milestones must be subject to Change Control.

The project schedule is developed in two key formats:

- Network diagram.
- Gantt (bar) chart.

Planning the project activities helps us to work out and clearly communicate what we need to do, who needs to do it, and in what order.

The schedule is effectively the project's time line or time plan. This is derived from the work packages defined in the work breakdown structure. There is a master schedule which gives the overall schedule of the project, identifies the major activities and key milestones. This is supported by more detailed schedules that highlight specific areas of the project. i.e. critical activities.

The precedence diagramming method: this method is also referred to as activity-on-node networks (AON networks) refers to a specific project management technique in which the project management team and or the project management team leader employs a network diagramming technique in order to represent any known and preexisting schedule activities via the use of boxes (which can also be referred to as nodes). Once all of these particular schedule activities have been displayed in a box, or node format, all of the individual boxes are linked together via the use of lines which represent any logical relationship (of if there are more than one, logical relationships) that are found to exist. The fundamental and most significant benefit to using the precedence diagramming method format technique is that it quickly and easily allows the project management team and or the project management team leader to view all schedule activities and their relationships with one another.

Earliest Start Time(EST)	Duration	Earliest Finish Time(EFT)
Task Identifier		
Latest Start Time(LST)	Total Float	Latest Finish Time(LFT)

Fig 15.1 Activity-on-Node notation

The information in the fully completed node is as follows:

- The duration (DUR) of each activity - how long it will take to complete.
- The earliest start time (EST) - the earliest an activity can start without interfering with the completion of any preceding activity.
- The latest start time (LST) - the latest an activity can start without interfering with the start of any subsequent activity.
- The earliest finish time (EFT) - the earliest an activity can finish.
- The latest finish time (LFT) - the latest an activity can finish without interfering with the start of any subsequent activity.
- The total "float" time of an activity - the time available to perform the activity less the time needed i.e. time available minus activity duration.

Many of the project planning software packages available use the Activity on node (AON) networks or Precedence Diagramming Method. This method plots the tasks to be completed and connects them with arrows that show the dependencies.

The sequence of work required to develop the schedule is as follows:

- Work out the dependencies - predecessors and successors.
- Draw the network diagram.

- Add the duration of each activity.

- Carry out a forward pass (from start to finish) through the network - filling in the earliest start and finish times - this enables a total project duration to be worked out.

- Carry out a backward pass (from finish back to start) - filling in the latest finish and start times - this enables the total float for each activity to be worked out (LST minus EST).

- Define the critical path (activities with zero total float when the total project duration has taken as the earliest finish time of the last activity). For activities on the critical path EST = LST.

This work will now be looked at in more detail; but note that the examination question on this topic **will no longer involve calculation**.

Mandatory dependencies are inherent in the work or process e.g. when constructing a new building, building the walls is dependent on first laying the foundations. Discretionary dependencies are those defined by the project manager and their team. They should be defined based on best practice or previous experience.

When drawing the precedence diagram, the project team needs to decide:

- which tasks can only be started after another task is completed;
- which tasks can be done at the same time.

  Examples of typical dependencies:

- finish to start - activity a must finish before activity b starts;
- start to start - activity b can only start when activity a has started;
- finish to finish - activity b can only finish when activity a has finished.

The usual convention is finish to start. There may however be exceptions where the plan calls for other links between tasks. All the links can be described in terms of a finish to start relationship in order to analyse the network.

Once the dependencies are agreed they can be mapped into a Network Diagram or Precedence Diagram.

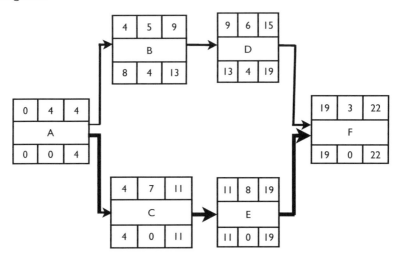

Figure 15.2 Example Network diagram

Diagram conventions:

- Connections between nodes must be shown as arrows.
- Arrows must always exit right and enter left of the node.

Many times the project duration is not the result of the project manager's estimates or even anyone else's calculations. It can be a deadline set by funders of the project or senior management as a wished for end date. It is only by doing these calculations that you can ascertain whether or not it is feasible to complete the project within the deadline.

Critical path is the term that is synonymous with project management. All project have a critical path, and some have more than one. A critical path will determine the shortest time in which a project can be completed. Another way of expressing this is to say that the critical path also represents the longest path of activity through the project. Both of these statements describe the significance of the critical path.

The reasons why the critical path is so important are:

- effort is focused on managing the activities that lie on the critical path because if all of them complete on time and if there is no slippage on other activities that exceeds their total float, the project will finish on time.

- the float on activities not on the critical path can be utilised to resolve resource scheduling problems.

Note that what is described as float in the UK is called slack in the USA.

The most common way of showing a project's schedule is to use a Gantt or bar chart as it is relatively simple to read and understand. A Gantt chart can be as simple as a list of activities drawn against a horizontal timescale, with each activity represented by a bar that also shows the period over which it is to be carried out; for small projects may be drawn on a spreadsheet.

The information contained within a project network diagram or a gantt chart for a project is the same: they are just different means of displaying the same information.

The **total float** is the time by which an activity may be delayed or extended without affecting the total project duration = LST minus EST. Total float is used to identify the critical path.

Once the schedule has been fully developed and included in the project management plan, it is said to be baselined. The baseline is the version of the schedule against which the project's time objectives will be monitored and controlled.

When preparing project schedules another key technique is the use of **milestones**. Milestones indicate key points in the schedule. Milestones represent the completion of deliverables or highlight key decision points on the project. They are not activities because they have zero duration.

Milestones can simplify the communication of the schedule by reporting the status of the project at a summary level. This kind of communication is essential for senior management or other parties who may not necessarily be interested in the detail of the project, but are interested in its outcome and progress. Milestones can also be used to set targets and monitor progress. Interim targets based on milestones can be established that can be monitored more closely than the multitude of activities that make up the project. Many organisations also use the completion of milestones as a means of determining when they pay their suppliers or contractors.

Gantt Charts

A Gantt chart is a bar chart representation of the network.

Each horizontal row represents an activity. The length of the horizontal bar corresponds to time and a calendar is drawn above the chart.

The following illustration is a representation of the previous network example:

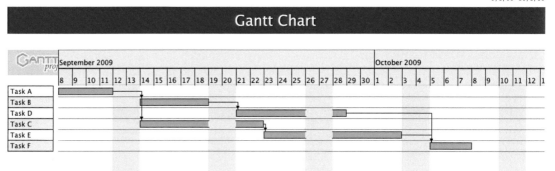

Figure 15.3 Gantt chart

This example has assumed no Saturday and Sunday working. Planning software for both networks and bar charts enables the project manager to set an electronic calendar based on working days, taking account of holiday periods.

In the above example, the task dependencies are shown by the arrow links and are easily seen. For a complex network these arrows could be more difficult to interpret.

Planning software can assist greatly in generating these charts. One example is GanttProject which is a cross-platform desktop tool for project scheduling and management. It runs on Windows, Linux and MacOSX; it is free and its code is open-source. It can:

- show a Gantt chart - Create work breakdown structure, draw dependencies, define milestones;
- show Resources - Assign human resources to work on tasks, see their allocation on the Resource Load chart;
- show PERT network chart - Generate PERT chart from Gantt chart;
- export - Save charts as PNG images, generate PDF and HTML reports;

- interoperate - Import projects from and export them to Microsoft Project formats. Export to spreadsheets with CSV;
- collaborate - Share projects with your colleagues using WebDAV.

Advantages of Gantt / bar charts:

- Provide an easy-to-read overview of the project.
- Relatively easy to construct.
- Interdependencies can be shown.
- Resource bar charts can be developed to manage the allocation of needed resources.
- Progress-tracking Gantt charts can be constructed.
- Easy to print as chart can be scaled to fit page.

Limitations:

Interdependencies of activities are not as apparent in this format as in the network diagram.

A Gantt with linked bars to show the interdependencies can become visually confusing in a larger project.

Milestone Progress Chart

A Milestone Progress Chart records milestone achievement and slippages and is used to forecast likely milestone achievement dates.

Milestones:

- are significant events / points of achievement in the project;
- have no duration, and use no resource;
- provide important progress monitoring and control points;
- are (key) review gates at the end of life cycle phases;
- are often related to payment / funding e.g. contractual or phased investment;

- are unambiguous – they are either achieved or not;
- can be clearly indicated on Gantt charts e.g. a 'diamond' symbol;

The chart is compiled as follows:

- The horizontal scale is the project calendar.
- The vertical scale shows the Monitoring period (reporting dates).
- The diagonal line is called the completion line - all completed milestones lie on this line.
- Milestone progress (achievement or slippage) is recorded on the chart on a regular basis by the project manager (e.g. weekly) by use of the different symbols (see key below chart).
- No milestone can appear below the line – it must either be already completed (on the line) or planned to be completed in the future (to the right of the line).

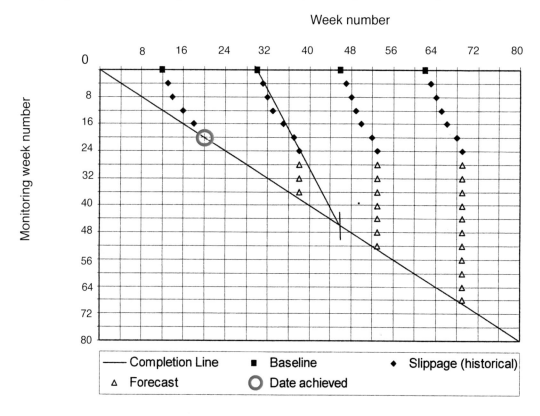

Figure 15.4 Milestone Progress Chart (after Lester 2007)

79

- On the example chart, we are currently in Monitoring Period 6, Week 24 of the project.
- This can be seen because the current status of the outstanding milestones are all shown on the line for Monitoring Period 6 - week 24.
- The expected milestone achievement dates (the clear triangles) are plotted on the chart, and where they intersect the diagonal line is their predicted achievement date.
- In the example, the predicted achievement dates presume that the slippage for all of the outstanding milestones will get no worse (e.g. the cause of the historical slippage has been resolved).
- The second milestone, for example, has currently slipped to around week 38. This is the present predicted achievement date, and unless we are given further information, we do not expect this to change over the next few Monitoring Periods. This is the optimistic view.

Advantages of the milestone progress chart:

- provides a clear view of the current status of milestone achievement and slippage;
- overcomes the ambiguity of % task complete – a milestone is either achieved or not;
- provides an historical record of milestone progress;
- can be used to forecast (through extrapolation) likely milestone achievement dates;
- extrapolation can be used to assess the impact of various milestone achievement scenarios (e.g. if a slippage is on or will feed into the critical path).

APM Sample Paper

Questions - 5, 50

Chapter 16 - Resource management and procurement

Assessment Criteria - assessment will require a learner to demonstrate that they can:

6.3 define resource management

6.5 list different categories and types of resources needed for projects

6.4 define procurement within the context of project management

16.1 Resource Management

Resource management comprises the acquisition and deployment of the internal and external resources required to deliver the project, programme or portfolio (BoK6)

Two types of resources are used:

- Consumable - when absent or consumed, fresh supplies are required e.g. money and materials - may be a product or a service.
- Re-usable - when no longer needed can be switched to other projects e.g. equipment, staff.

There are three steps in the process:

- Allocation - identifying what resources are needed for each activity.
- Aggregation - often shown in a histogram on a daily, weekly or monthly basis.
- Scheduling - limited availability of resources usually means that the schedule has to be altered to match availability of the resources.

16.2 Resource scheduling

Resource scheduling is a collection of techniques used to calculate the resources required to deliver the work and when they will be required. (BoK 6).

Effective resource scheduling ensures:

- efficient use of resources;
- confidence that the schedule is realistic in terms of available resources;
- early identification of potential bottlenecks and conflicts in the use of potential resources.

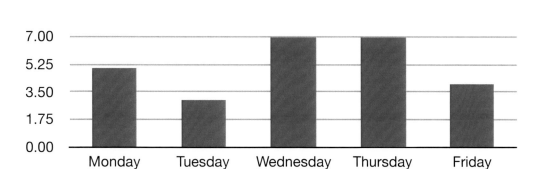

Required Resource

Figure 16.1 Histogram of resource requirement

Assume that the above histogram represents usage of staff on a project - only five people are available each day. Resource scheduling has to be carried out.

Techniques of resource scheduling are:

- Resource smoothing.
- Resource levelling.

Resource smoothing

Resource smoothing (or time-limited scheduling) aims to ensure that resources are used as efficiently as possible. The duration of the project remains constant but resources are switched between time periods to smooth out peaks and troughs in the histogram. This is limited by the amount of float on activities within the project. Smoothing reduces the amplitudes of the peaks and troughs but does not remove them completely. In the example, additional resource has to be made available to complete the activity on Friday.

Resource levelling

Resource levelling (or resource-limited scheduling) is applied when there are limits on the availability of resource - which is being exceeded. Resources are delayed and if delayed beyond the limits of the float, will result in delay to completion of the project. In the example, activities are rescheduled within the float but the project has to be extended into the following week for completion.

16.3 Procurement

Procurement is the process by which products and services are acquired from an external provider for incorporation into the project, programme or portfolio (BoK6)

Procurement usually involves the use of a legal contract to acquire the required goods or services - a most important activity handled in bigger organisations by a purchasing or contracts department.

APM Sample Paper

Questions - 20, 34

Chapter 17 - Issues and change control

Assessment Criteria - assessment will require a learner to demonstrate that they can:

7.6 define an issue

7.7 define issue management

7.8 explain the difference between an issue and a risk

7.9 describe the use of an issue log

5.4A define the following in relation to scope management - change control

5.6 list the steps involved in a typical change control process

17.1 Issue management

An issue is a threat to the project objectives that cannot be resolved by the project manager. (BoK 5)

A formal issue occurs when the tolerances of delegated work are predicted to be exceeded or have been exceeded. This triggers the escalation of the issue from one level of management to the next in order to find a solution. (BoK 6)

So the definition has broadened from BoK 5 to BoK 6. The BoK 5 definition is just part of that in BoK 6.

Issues are differentiated from problems, which are concerns that the manager deals with on a day-to-day basis within delegated responsibilities. Issues are outside the envelope of delegated authority and must be escalated, whereas problems are within the direct control of the manager or project manager and can be managed without escalating.

Note that an issue to those to whom the work has been delegated by the Project Manager may be just a problem to the project manager.

Risks and issues are also differentiated in that risks are uncertain events that may or may not occur, whereas issues have already occurred or are certain to occur and are therefore no longer uncertain - the uncertainty has disappeared.

The importance of issue management for the project manager is that issues are outside their direct control. The project manager must ensure that issues are escalated to the appropriate authority (project sponsor, project board etc.) so that they can be resolved.

Issues are captured in an issue log (issue register) so they can be tracked and resolved. The issue log also contains a record of what happens and the decision taken to address the issue. This is issue management.

The process applied to Project Issues is similar to the process for change control (see the next section). The process is differentiated by the incorporation of the escalation process.

The issue management process has five steps:

- **Capture**
- **Evaluate**
- **Escalate**
- **Resolve**
- **Monitor**

During the first stage, all issues are captured and recorded in the issue log or register.

The issue information that is recorded includes:

- date when the Issue was first raised;
- reference number (a unique reference number is provided for each Issue);
- status of the Issue (open or closed);
- description (the full description of the Issue);
- author (the name of the person who has raised the Issue);
- impact (possible consequences or impacts on the project);
- possible resolution (options for resolving the Issue);
- final outcome (how the Issue was eventually resolved);
- date closed.

The Resolution Owner will provide regular updates on the status of the Issue. The Issue Log is updated to reflect the status of the monitoring. The frequency of the reports depends on the severity and urgency of the Issue.

The process of dealing with Issues forms part of the Project Initiation Document or Project Management Plan.

Within this process, the roles and responsibilities for Issue Management are defined.

17.2 Change control

Change control is the process through which all requests to change the baseline scope of the project, programme or portfolio are captured, evaluated and then approved, rejected or deferred. (BoK 6)

The main purpose of change control is to ensure that the changes to the specification or scope of a project do not result in the project failing. Therefore, change control is a process that is implemented by the project manager in order to maintain the business case and the project management plan throughout the phases of the project life cycle. Having such a process in place facilitates assessment of the impact, cost and importance of potential changes and enables a decision to be made on whether or not to include the change.

This process begins at the point when a change is requested. It then goes through a decision making stage i.e. whether to implement the change or not and it concludes with communication and documentation of the result of the decisions. Change control may appear bureaucratic however, the impact of unmanaged project changes has a greater effect.

Project changes usually occur for the following reasons:

A. From the Project Team

- Personnel changes.
- Use of new technologies and tools.

- Increased use of staff resources.

- Discovery of error in design or estimation.

It was reported in May 2014 that French railway operator SNCF had ordered hundreds of new trains that turned out too wide to fit alongside all the regional platforms. SNCF's failure to verify measurements resulted in an extra cost of €50m to modify 1,300 platforms in one in six regional stations.

B. From the Client

- Scope creep or scope leap - we need 40% more office space!

- Personnel changes.

- Variation orders - work additional to main contract and separately funded.

C. From the external environment

- Mandatory changes from new regulations.

- Unavailability of resources, such as cranes for construction of tall buildings.

Change Control Plan

During the project planning phase, the project manager is responsible for developing the change control plan as part of the PMP. This is to ensure a disciplined approach within the implementation phase to dealing with the requests for changes to the frozen project management plan.

One of the main responsibilities of a project manager during the third or development phase of a project is the application and administration of formal change control.

Project change requests are recorded, evaluated, authorised and managed through project change control. Without this the project scope may increase and may affect the cost and possibly the project deadline. A project that costs more and takes longer may not achieve its success criteria and thus not meet its business case.

A formal change control process has five main stages:

- recording of the proposed change (**capture**)
- evaluation or impact assessment (**evaluate**)
- authorisation or rejection (**recommend and decide**)
- update plans (**communicate**) and
- management (**implement**).

A. Capture

Proposed project changes are usually documented on a change request form and then recorded (logged) in a change log (change register).

The change request form should include:

- Date when change request was raised.
- A unique reference number for the change request.
- Who requested the change.
- A description of the change request.

All these requested changes must be recorded in the change log. It lists all project changes whatever their status: proposed, authorised, rejected or deferred. Change logs can be created as a table using word-processing software or a spreadsheet or a database that lists key aspects of a change. These include in addition to the data on the change request form:

- Impact assessment.
- Priority assessment - based on the assessed impact.
- Decision - authorised, declined or deferred.
- Date when a decision was made.
- Allocation details - details of whom the request for change has been allocated to.

B. Evaluate

Each request for change should be evaluated by an impact analysis. In some cases an initial evaluation may be done in order to ascertain whether it is worthwhile doing a detailed evaluation. Detailed evaluation may in itself cause additional costs which may affect the frozen PMP.

Detailed evaluations should consider the impact the request for change will have on:

- the project objectives in terms of time, cost, quality and scope;
- the safety aspects of the change;
- the project business case, especially in terms of the impact on benefits;
- the project risk profile, i.e. the impact on the overall risk exposure of the project.

Based on the analysis of the above an assessment can then be made as to the priority of the request for change; is it considered to be a must, important nice to have, cosmetic?

In addition it needs to be clarified whether additional funds are required that cannot be obtained from any reserve held by the project manager.

This evaluation may be passed to a Change Control Board and/or the project team. The Change Control Board is made up of representatives from various parts of the project organisation. If it is approved by them, it is passed to the steering group (or Project Board) for a final decision.

C. Recommend and Decide

Requests for change should be brought to the attention of the steering group (or Project Board) in an Exception Report. This contains the following information:

- Description of the request for change.
- Consequence of the request for change.
- Available options.

- Effect of each option on the time, cost, quality and scope; the business case; and the risks.
- Project Manager's recommendation.

The options are to approve, reject or defer the change request.

D. Communicate

Once approved any changes must be brought to the attention of the relevant stakeholders. The project team must be fully informed of the changes. The person requesting the change should be also be informed of the outcome of the process .

E. Implementation

After a decision to authorise a request for change, plans are updated to reflect the change. In addition the actions required to implement the change are then taken. The change log is updated to record the decision that has been made.

Project managers find an up to date change log invaluable both during and after the project. During the project it helps in understanding the changes that are in the pipeline and their potential impact on the project. After the project, it allows the project manager to explain if necessary any deviation from the expected outcome. For example why the project cost more or less, why the project took more or less time or any variance in project deliverables.

Changes that are authorised must be managed. This includes updating the project management plan (PMP) including the project schedule, budget etc. Once this is done the change request is considered closed.

In some cases a 'change freeze' may have to be imposed - during which no new requests for changes will be considered. This may occur if it is felt that operation of the change control process may delay the completion date of the project or cause extra costs through evaluation.

APM Sample Paper

Questions - 4, 21, 35, 48

Chapter 18 - Configuration management

Assessment Criteria - assessment will require a learner to demonstrate that they can:

5.4(B) define the following in relation to scope management - configuration management

5.5 explain the relationship between change control and configuration management

5.7 list the activities in a typical configuration management process

18.1 Configuration management

Configuration management encompasses the administrative activities concerned with the creation, maintenance, controlled change and quality control of the scope of the work. (BoK 6)

There are two important words in this definition - 'configuration' and 'scope'.

Scope was defined in chapter 13 - *the totality of the outputs, outcomes and benefits and the work required to produce them (BoK 6).*

The basic meaning of the word 'configuration' is the layout of components within an output. Within project management, the word has extra meaning as shown in the APM BoK 6 definition (above). It includes much detail on each component (eg test results, supplier, etc - very important in a safety-conscious industry such as the rail industry). Thus Configuration Management administers the records of the configuration and in particular any alterations to the configuration.

Note that configuration management is required during the detailed design process whilst the baseline version is being developed and improved, and secondly, later in the third phase of the lifecycle whilst the deliverables are being constructed.

Configuration describes the totality of the different elements of the project that need to be controlled. These elements can be physical things or largely intangible. Each of these is called a configuration item and is identified through configuration identification. Configuration items have a specific purpose and a unique identification which is then controlled through configuration management.

Version control or revision control is part of the configuration management process, which is important throughout the project life cycle.

Change control and configuration management are usually linked as an authorised project change often results in at least one configuration item being updated.

The key aspect of Configuration Management and Change Control is the ability to identify and control different versions of a product. For example some software is available in three versions - a student or basic version, a platinum or top-level version and one in-between maybe called a professional version. Upgrades to the software require careful recording of the features in each version.

Therefore, Configuration Management is needed to identify, track and protect the project's outputs.

- Identify: ensure that each product and each version of a product is uniquely identified.
- Track: information is maintained for each product relating to its status, ownership and relationship with other products.
- Protect: no product can be altered without authorised agreement from change control.

18.2 The Configuration Management Process

There are five activities (or functions) within Configuration Management:

- Planning
- Identification
- Control
- Status accounting
- Audit

A. Configuration Management Planning

This involves planning the level of configuration management required by the project and how this will be achieved. This forms the Configuration Management Plan which is part of the Project Management Plan.

One of the ways to decide the level of configuration management is by using a Product Breakdown Structure down to the level of configuration items. The Configuration Management plan defines:

- how the items and the various versions of these will be identified;
- roles and responsibility for carrying out configuration management, particularly who may authorise any changes;
- where the libraries and files are to be held.

The production of the plan and performing configuration management can be delegated from the project manager to a configuration librarian.

B. Configuration Identification

This involves breakdown of the product into its configuration items (or component parts) with their specification and identification.

The coding system identifies the following:

- The project in which the item is created.
- Type of item and item title.
- Identification number of item.
- Latest version number.
- Owner.
- Library or location where it is kept.
- Links to related items.
- Status of the item.
- Copyholders and potential users.

C. Configuration Control

This is about controlling the addition of approved changes to a version of the design. The changes from change control are documented and incorporated in new baseline designs, which are internally consistent. In configuration management terms, a baseline is a snapshot of a product and any component items, frozen usually at stages of the design or construction process e.g. the beginning of the third phase of the lifecycle or after a design freeze. As the design progresses, new and more detailed baseline versions may be created. If the product that has been baselined is to be changed then a new version of the baseline is created to accommodate the change and the baseline version remains unchanged. Old baseline versions are never discarded, so there is a record of all versions used.

A release is a related concept e.g. a beta-version of operating system software. This is a complete and consistent set of products that form a fixed reference point in the development of the end product.

D. Configuration status accounting

This is the recording and reporting of all current and historic information concerning each product ie records and logs the approved changes to the baselines as well as providing traceability of all configuration items throughout the project. The record will also contain records of any change requests which are in the pipeline.

For example, records have to be kept of which deliverables contain components from which supplier. Thus a car serial number accesses a list of exactly which components are in a particular car.

E. Configuration audit

This is the review process that ensures the actual status of all products matches the authorised state of products as per the configuration management records. These reviews audit the products against the Configuration Item Records in order to identify any discrepancies and checks that the configuration management process is in accordance with the Configuration Management Plan. Reviews are usually undertaken at the end of each stage and at the end of the project.

APM Sample Paper

Question - 51

Chapter 19 - Information management and reporting

Assessment Criteria - assessment will require a learner to demonstrate that they can:

4.13 define the purpose and benefits of project reporting

19.1 Information management

Information Management is the collection, storage, dissemination, archiving and destruction of information. It enables teams and stakeholders to use their time, resource and expertise effectively to make decisions and fulfil their roles. (BoK 6)

Projects generate, utilise and absorb significant quantities of information.

Information is therefore collected to provide a repository of information for the project, and a means of controlling information flow. Information may need to be actively sought, rather than being automatically delivered into the project.

Decisions are made as to what information is appropriate to store, how to store it so that it can be readily accessed/retrieved by the relevant people or systems. Information that is collected but does not need to be stored is destroyed as per agreed procedures. Careful consideration should be given to the destruction of information; for example, can paper be recycled or must it be destroyed in order to protect confidentiality?

Dissemination involves the distribution of existing information and the conversion of data to information for distribution.

Information is archived throughout the project life cycle. This allows for information to be removed from immediately accessible storage to an archive therefore it is no longer readily accessible.

Information management changes during the project life cycle in terms of understanding what is needed, who to disseminate information to, when to issue information and when to destroy it. The information required must adhere to the communication plan.

Other factors such as commercial confidentiality and statutory obligations such as information security and freedom of information should also be considered. Information management in a project needs to integrate with the organisation's information management process.

A decision must be made as to the required detail that should be collected, stored and archived. In addition the use to which information will be put post-project should be considered. It will be the case that some information generated during the project will be beneficial to the organisation in its following business-as-usual activities and when undertaking similar projects.

The Government Construction Strategy for Building Information Modelling (BIM) was published by the Cabinet office on 31 May 2011. The report announced the Governments intention to require collaborative 3-D BIM (with all project and asset information, documentation and data being electronic) on its projects by 2016. So watch out for terms such as 'Employers Information Requirements' and ' BIM Execution Plan'.

19.2 Reporting

Reporting is the process by which stakeholders are kept informed about the project as included in the communication plan.

Project reporting is reporting on the status of the project. This is one of the main duties of the Project Manager. Project reporting takes information about the project and presents it in an appropriate format to the stakeholders and is in line with the communication plan. The term "reporting" implies that most report are written; however, reports can be verbal via progress meetings or conference calls.

Reporting tends to be a formal process with reports issued or presented as per the following criteria:

- in line with an agreed calendar (e.g. weekly, or monthly);
- at predetermined points in the life cycle (e.g. at the end of each phase or after significant activity has taken place).

Reports cover topics such as progress against schedule, expenditure against the budget and performance against the quality plan, the latest predicted end date and also against agreed key performance indicators (KPI's). Report are also produced as a result of audits, project reviews and risk assessments.

These reports give an indiction of whether the project will deliver the required bene-fits, if there is underperformance the action can be taken to rectify this.

One of the techniques employed is reporting by exception. Therefore, if everything is going to plan then almost nothing is said or written. Only when things are not going to plan i.e. things are ahead or behind schedule, there is under or over spending, quality is better or worse than planned that a report is made. This form or reporting is intended to reduce the burden of reporting and requires trust between project manager and stake-holder that no news is good news and anything to the contrary will be reported and therefore requires attention.

APM Sample Paper

Question - 23

Chapter 20 - Communication

Assessment Criteria - assessment will require a learner to demonstrate that they can:

9.1 define communication

9.2 outline different media of communication; outline potential barriers to effective communication

9.3 identify ways to facilitate effective communication

9.4 define the contents of a communication plan

9.5 explain the benefits of a communication plan

20.1 Communication

Communication is the means by which information or instructions are exchanged. Successful communication occurs when the received meaning is the same as the transmitted meaning. (BoK 6)

What Is Communication?

Communication is defined as a process by which we assign and convey meaning in an attempt to create shared understanding. This process requires a vast repertoire of skills in intrapersonal and interpersonal processing, listening, observing, speaking, questioning, analysing, and evaluating. Use of these processes is developmental and transfers to all areas of life: home, school, community, work, and beyond. It is through communication that collaboration and co-operation occur.

20.2 The Communication Process

Effective communication is about conveying your message clearly and unambiguously. It is also about receiving information from others with as little distortion as possible. The communication process is illustrated below:

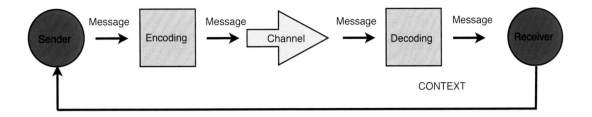

Fig 20.1 The Communications Process

Any one of these stages provides the potential for misunderstanding and confusion. An effective communicator gets their point across without misunderstanding or confusion and aims to lessen the frequency of problems at each stage of this process with well planned communication that is clear, concise and accurate.

Stages of the communication process

- Source: Person generating the message. Clarity is require about why you are communicating and what you are communicating. The information you communicate needs to be useful and accurate.

- Message: The information you want to communicate.

- Encoding: Putting the message in a form that can be sent and correctly decoded at the other end. Success at this stage is dependent on your ability to anticipate and eliminate sources of confusion e.g. mistaken assumptions, cultural issues and missing information. This stage is also dependent on you knowing your audience and your ability to convey information clearly and simply.

- Channel: The method of delivery of the message. The verbal channel includes face-to-face meeting, telephone and videoconferencing; written channels include letter, emails, texts, memos and reports. Each channel has strengths and weaknesses. E.g. long lists of direction are not effective orally or negative feedback by e-mail is not effective.

- Decoding: This skill requires either taking the time to read the message carefully or actively listening to it in order to avoid decoding errors. These errors usually arise if the decoder does not have enough knowledge to understand the message or misread or misheard the message.

- Receiver: The message is delivered to an individual or group. You have in mind a set of actions or reactions that your message will get. Be aware that each individual enters into the communications process with ideas and feelings that usually influence their understanding of your message and their response.

- Feedback: You audience will provide feedback, this is either verbal or nonverbal reactions to your message. Paying attention to this feedback will inform you whether your message has been understood or to clear up any misunderstanding.

- Context: The situation in which your message is delivered is the context - includes the surrounding environment or broader culture eg corporate or international culture.

Effective Communication

Effective communication is a two-way process - sending the right message, that is also being correctly received and understood by the other person/s.

For communication to be effective, it is important to understand how the people you are interacting with may interpret your message. We obtain information through our senses, and it is therefore recommended that your communication includes aspects of the visual, auditory and kinaesthetic language to appeal to all listeners. Kinaesthetic means the sensation by which bodily position, weight, muscle tension, and movement are perceived. Kinaesthetic learning means learning by doing.

Communication is defined as a process by which we assign and convey meaning in an attempt to create shared understanding. This process requires a vast repertoire of skills in intrapersonal and interpersonal processing, listening, observing, speaking, questioning, analysing and evaluating. It is through communication that collaboration and cooperation occur. Thus, communication is the means for sharing ideas, feelings and resources. Communication breakdown, disagreements and misunderstandings are immediately apparent. However, this skill is taken for granted. The underlying assumption is that speaking the same language only requires effort and sincerity to communicate successfully. This ignores the impact of emotions, motivation, intelligence, risk-taking to name some of the issues.

20.3 Communication Plan

Effective communication is the key to project success and is arguably one of the most important activities for project success.

The project manager needs to ensure that there are lines of communication:

- with and between the project team members;
- between the project team and other stakeholders.

A communications plan identifies what information is to be communicated to whom, why, when, where, how, through which medium and the desired impact. This is developed as part of the project management plan (PMP). It is also linked to the responsibility assignment matrix (RAM) and the stakeholder management plan.

The communication plan includes the following (APM Pathways):

- Executive summary.
- Key messages (mission, vision, goals, activities etc.).
- Audience (team members, senior management, other departments, contractors, other stakeholders).
- Communication methods/media (face-to-face, team briefings, minutes, memos, e-mail, websites, blogs etc).
- Feedback routes (communications methods/media, contact points etc.).
- Responsibilities (maintenance of document distribution schedule, contact points from RAM, authorship etc.).
- Measurement (feedback on effectiveness of communication plan/monitor and control mechanism).
- Timing of communications.

20.4 Barriers to Communication

Barriers may be grouped according to the communication process:

A. Sender/Receiver - Personal factors.
B. Encoding/Decoding - Use of english as the language.

C. Channel - Technical barriers.

D. Context - Workplace factors.

A. Personal Factors of the sender and receiver

The following can cause psychological barriers:

- Timing - Message should be delivered at a time that is most effective.

- Style and tone - This is largely down to perception.

- Non-verbal - Appearance, body language.

- Lack of mutual respect - The perceived inequalities of position or competence of receiver and sender.

- Interpersonal differences - Individual differences of team members.

- Importance - Message disregarded as unimportant by recipient.

- Selective listening - The filtering of information.

- Received wisdom and conformity - The resistance to different ways of doing things.

- Perception - The interpretation of information based on our knowledge and experience.

B. Encoding/Decoding

- English Language - Technical terms (jargon), pronunciation, poor grammar, spelling and punctuation.

C. Technical Barriers associated with the channel

These are the practical reasons that could make a message difficult to understand.

- Geographic - Time differences can make it difficult to converse.

- Structure - The information is structured poorly or illogically.

- Unclear/faint print - Poor photocopies, faxes or partially delivered text messages or e-mail.

- Equipment problems - Bad transmission on a mobile or malfunctioning equipment.

- Lost documents - Lost post or undelivered e-mails can lead to the assumption that information was received though not acknowledged.

- Information or message overload - Too many e-mails or methods of communication can lead to messages being missed or forgotten.

- The method - Choose the method that is appropriate to the desired outcome - letter, e-mail, phone call etc.

D. The context

- Cultural differences - These can be national, organisational, departmental or cultural.
- Seniority differences in workplace - Status and authority can inhibit others.
- Political - Hidden agendas, filtered information, perceived alliances.

Remember that it is essential for communication to be two-way through out the project. Therefore the listening and speaking are just as important as the project managers ability to be understood! i.e. the way in which he or she conveys information.

Nonverbal Behaviors of Communication

To deliver the full impact of a message, use non-verbal behaviors to raise the channel of interpersonal communication:

- **Eye contact**: This helps to regulate the flow of communication. It signals interest in others and increases the speaker's credibility. People who make eye contact open the flow of communication and convey interest, concern, warmth, and credibility.

- **Facial Expressions**: Smiling is a powerful cue that transmits happiness, friendliness, warmth, and liking. So, if you smile frequently you will be perceived as more likable, friendly, warm and approachable. Smiling is often contagious and people will react favorably. They will be more comfortable around you and will want to listen more.

- **Gestures**: If you fail to gesture while speaking you may be perceived as boring and stiff. A lively speaking style captures the listener's attention, makes the conversation more interesting, and facilitates understanding.

- **Posture and body orientation**: You communicate numerous messages by the way you talk and move. Standing erect and leaning forward communicates to listeners that you are approachable, receptive and friendly. Interpersonal closeness results when you and the listener face each other. Speaking with your back turned or looking at the floor or ceiling should be avoided as it communicates disinterest.

- **Proximity**: Cultural norms dictate a comfortable distance for interaction with others. You should look for signals of discomfort caused by invading the other person's space. Some of these are: rocking, leg swinging, tapping, and gaze aversion.

- **Vocal**: Speaking can signal nonverbal communication when you include such vocal elements as: tone, pitch, rhythm, timbre, loudness, and inflection. For maximum teaching effectiveness, learn to vary these six elements of your voice. One of the major criticisms of many speakers is that they speak in a monotone voice. Listeners perceive this type of speaker as boring and dull.

20.5 Mehrabian and the 7%-38%-55% Myth

We often hear that the content of a message is composed of:

- 55% from the visual component - the facial expression;
- 38% from the auditory component - the way the words are said;
- 7% from language - the words that are spoken.

However, the above percentages only apply in a very narrow context - **to communications of feelings and attitudes (i.e. like/dislike)**. Mehrabian was interested in how listeners get their information about a speaker's general attitude in situations where the facial expression, tone, and/or words are sending conflicting signals. He wasn't asking about the words at all, but rather the speaker's intent.

Thus, he designed a couple of experiments. In one, Mehrabian and Ferris (1967) researched the interaction of speech, facial expressions, and tone. Three different speakers were instructed to say "maybe" with three different attitudes towards their listener (positive, neutral, or negative). Next, photographs of the faces of three female models were taken as they attempted to convey the emotions of like, neutrality, and dislike.

Test groups were then instructed to listen to the various renditions of the word "maybe," with the pictures of the models, and were asked to rate the attitude of the speaker. Note that the emotion and tone were often mixed, such as a facial expression showing dislike, with the word "maybe" spoken in a positive tone.

Mehrabian discovered if your body language and tone of voice didn't match your words, when you were talking about feelings and attitudes, the audience would tend to believe your non-verbal communication and tonality of voice.

His big insight was that when words and non-verbal messages are in conflict, people believe the non-verbal every time. So if you are dealing with someone worse the wear for drink and thus perhaps not very good at focussing or estimating distance, any approach towards them may appear threatening. It is of less importance what you say - however helpful - it is the visual message that is received.

APM Sample Paper

Questions - 1, 17, 30

Chapter 21 - Roles and responsibilities

Assessment Criteria - assessment will require a learner to demonstrate that they can:

3.1 define the roles and responsibilities of:

★   project manager

★   project sponsor

★   project steering group/board

★   project team members

★   project office

★   end users

21.1 Organisational roles

Organisational roles are the roles performed by individuals or groups in a project. Both roles and responsibilities within projects must be defined to address the transient and unique nature of projects and to ensure that clear accountabilities can be assigned. (APM BoK 5th edition)

Steering Group/Board - may also be called steering committee or project board - provides overall strategic direction to the project. Chaired by the Sponsor and consists of representatives from the users, suppliers and stakeholders.

The Project Sponsor - owns the business case, is responsible for achieving the benefits specified in the business case, accountable for the project. If no steering group then the sponsor provides the strategic direction.

The Project Manager - manages the project on a day-to-day basis, responsible for delivering the capability that allows the benefits to be realised - *must be competent in managing the six aspects of a project - scope, schedule, finance, risk, quality and resources. Well-developed interpersonal skills such as leadership, communication and conflict management are also vitally important.* (BoK 6)

The Project Team members - accountable to the project manager

Project Office Team - provides support to the project manager and to the sponsor.

Users - represents those who will benefit from the project. They may be subject matter experts and contribute to defining requirements and acceptance criteria.

Suppliers/Contractors - represents those who will supply resources to the project. They can be internal or external to the organisation.

Stakeholders - those with an interest in the project, contribute to defining requirements, quality.

21.2 Project sponsorship

Project sponsorship is an active senior management role. The sponsor is accountable for ensuring that the work is governed effectively and delivers the objectives that meet identified needs. (BoK6)

Projects implement change and that allows organisations to fulfil their business objectives. This emphasises the benefits realisation, rather than delivery of deliverables. Consequently the role of the sponsor is to direct a project with benefits in mind, as opposed to the project manager, who managers the project with delivery in mind with consideration of the benefits to be realised. Project sponsorship is therefore more pertinent to project effectiveness while project management is more concerned with project efficiency.

A sponsor may also be referred to as the project executive (PRINCE2), senior responsible officer, project director, project champion or project owner.

The sponsor is the primary risk taker and owner of the project's business case. The sponsor is tasked with ensuring that the benefits of a project are realised and therefore needs to ensure that any obstacles faced by a project are dealt with.

There should only be one sponsor per project. The sponsor often chairs the steering group and is the person to whom the project manager is accountable. The relationship between sponsor and project manager is based on continuous dialogue, with a common understanding of the project context, the benefits sought and the costs and risks of achieving those benefits.

The steering group oversees a project and provides strategic guidance. This group is also referred to as the steering committee or project board.

Without clear goals, direction and business leadership provided by the sponsor even the best project manager and project team can struggle to succeed. Similarly, without clear, timely decisions and support a project will falter.

Responsibilities of the Sponsor to the Board

- Provides leadership on culture and values.
- Owns the business case.
- Keeps project aligned with organisation's strategy and portfolio direction.
- Governs project risk.
- Works with other sponsors.
- Focuses on realisation of benefits.
- Recommends opportunities to optimise cost/benefits.
- Ensures continuity of sponsorship.
- Provides assurance that governance arrangements and policies are being applied.
- Provides feedback and lessons learnt.

What the Sponsor does for the Project Manager

- Provides timely decisions.
- Clarifies decision-making framework.
- Clarifies business priorities and strategy.
- Communicates business issues.
- Provides resources.
- Engenders trust.
- Manages relationships.
- Supports the project manager's role.
- Promotes ethical working.

Activities during the project life cycle

Concept phase

- Establish project context with the Project Manager.
- Confirm the Project Team.

111

- Ensure adequate resources are available for the project.

- State the required benefits for inclusion in the Business Case.

- Sign off the Business Case.

- Apply to the Board for permission to proceed with the definition phase.

Definition phase

- Authorise the Project Manager to proceed with the definition phase.

- Provide guidance to the Project Manager during preparation of the Project Management Plan (PMP).

- Apply to the Board for permission to proceed with the development phase.

Development phase

- Authorise the Project Manager to proceed with the development phase.

- Support the Project Manager.

- Deal with Change requests.

- Arrange to realise the benefits.

Handover and closure phase

- Accept the deliverables after checking they meet the acceptance criteria.

- Complete arrangements for benefits realisation.

- Take part in the post-project review and sign off the final project reports.

After Project Closure

- Organise the Benefit Realisation Review(s)

APM Sample Paper

Questions - 12, 13, 26, 56

Chapter 22 - What makes a good project manager?

No Assessment Criteria

22.1 Introduction

APM defines project management as the application of processes, methods, knowledge, skills and experience to achieve the project objectives. So the most important aspect of the project manager role is to manage the project in order to achieve the project objectives - to deliver the capability that allows the benefits to be realised.

BoK 6 also says that the project manager "*is responsible for day-to-day management of the project and must be competent in managing the six aspects of a project - scope, schedule, finance, risk, quality and resources. Well-developed interpersonal skills such as leadership, communication and conflict management are also vitally important.*"

The earlier parts of this study guide related to managing these six aspects of a project. In this chapter we start to tackle the interpersonal skills. So it seems sensible to discuss what perceptions people have about the required attributes of a project manager.

In his book on Project Management, Paul Gardiner refers to a survey of project leadership skills. Project managers in the USA and UK were asked to list in order of importance the key attributes of a project manager - based on a list of 26 skills. The results showed a clear difference between the responses from excellent project managers (the top 2% who always seemed to complete their projects on time) and average project managers. Average project managers rated highly:

- to have a sound technical knowledge,

- to pay attention to detail,

- to be imaginative and creative.

The excellent project managers rated highly:

- to be conscious of the political aspects,

- to assume ownership for the mission.

The excellent project managers seem happy to delegate some of the skills to members of the project team. We will see these skills re-appearing in chapter 25 in the descriptions of the Belbin team roles. The excellent project managers seem to concentrate primarily on those skills that cannot be delegated.

22.2 Competence Framework

Demonstration of a competence shows an ability to perform an activity to a required standard. Thus a project manager's job may be defined in terms of required competences.

In 2008 APM published its Competence Framework. The second edition was published in June 2015 bringing it up-to-date.

In developing the new framework, APM has simplified and improved the format to make it easier to understand and use. APM describe the new features as:

- *"Each competence defines what the practitioner actually needs to be able to do. 'Introductory notes' provide a summary and describe its place in the context of the wider project management framework.*

- *Duplication between the competences has been removed and the number of competences refined from 47 to 27.*

- *14 role profiles have also been developed, which identify the subset of competences that apply to individual roles.*

- *A specific focus on programme management, portfolio management and the PMO, including role profiles, make it a modern resource that meets the needs of today's project professionals.*

- *Each competence also has indicators for both 'knowledge' and 'application', allowing the assessment to evaluate both of these factors.*

- *The scoring matrix has been refined to a five-point scale."*

Chapter 23 - Motivation

No Assessment Criteria

23.1 Motivation

Managing people requires an understanding of motivation. It has been suggested that individuals are motivated to satisfy different needs at different times. The first requirements are to meet basic survival needs; once these are satisfied then we are able to work towards achieving growth and creating meaning. It is the drive to fulfill the needs for survival and growth which leads to overcoming feelings of fear and limitation.

Fig 23.1 Maslow's Hierarchy of needs

Maslow's hierarchy of needs proposes that individual needs affect behaviour in accord with two principles:

- The Deficit Principle: A satisfied need is not a motivator of behaviour. People act to satisfy unfilled needs - a satisfaction deficit.
- The Progression Principle: A need only becomes activated once the lower needs have been satisfied.

The basic premise is that those who are hungry or without shelter will strive to satisfy these needs before paying attention to the others. In other words the most dominant behaviour highlights an unsatisfied need. i.e. someone under financial pressure or in poor health is likely to pay less attention to team relationships and will be less creative. Therefore the core idea here is the impact of needs on motivation and performance.

Team goals are achieved by recognising individual members starting points and building on this as satisfaction of needs contributes directly to improved performance for the team.

There are of course exceptions. As a result this theory has been criticised. An example of an exception is someone who ignores lower needs whilst striving for esteem or self-actualisation. In other words this is a good guideline for the identification of how needs will affect motivation - however, the order may not apply to everyone.

Types of Rewards

In order for reward to be an effective motivator, the benefit that people derive from their jobs has to be obvious (i.e. what need does the reward satisfy)

Three types of rewards:

- Incentive (carrots).
- Threats (stick).
- Intrinsic (job satisfaction).

Incentives (carrots)

These carrots may be money, a bigger car, larger office, share options; basically things that can be given to the individual as a reward for doing a good job.

Pay is the most commonly used incentive. However, its value as a motivator tends to depend on the person so can be limited. People often value other aspects of their work more highly than the monetary reward.

Annual pay increase (usually inflation linked) - this is an expected outcome therefore does not necessarily motivate to work harder.

Performance-related pay increases or bonuses are often used to motivate. There is however, a risk with this approach as there is the possibility of the individual feeling that the amount given does not accurately reflect the effort invested.

There may be occasions where additional payments are needed to achieve a task e.g. overtime payments to expedite an activity on the project schedule. There are many organisations that do not award overtime payments to management personnel.

Frederick Herzberg postulated that these carrots are hygiene factors. Hygiene factors do not deliver job satisfaction, rather they act as 'dissatisfiers' when absent (e.g. pay for the job is perceived to be inadequate) and are sources of job dissatisfaction

Threats (sticks)

These are rules that are backed up by penalties and or punishment. Examples of these are disciplinary procedure or in a project management context liquidated damages in a supply contract. Rules are considered effective as they motivate people "away from punishment". So to keep their job they obey the rules.

Rules are limited in their motivational effect as they may create an environment where the minimum effort required to stay within the rules is exerted. So it is possible to get by without engaging or performing at your best.

Threats that are aimed at maximizing performance are ineffective on a long term basis as it can create a culture of fear where problems are not openly discussed and under performance is hidden or blamed on others. The resulting fear culture can become highly political, with blame culture, etc which leads to an unpleasant environment which usually results in the loss of star performers.

The use of stick appropriately in combination with other methods can be effective as under-performance needs to be tackled quickly and decisively to avoid it become disruptive to the team or organisation. For example a project manager would be required to tackle an under-performing team member as in this context it can jeopardise the delivery of a project.

117

Intrinsic Motivation

This is internal motivation - the pleasure that one gets from the task itself or from the sense of satisfaction of working on the task or completing the task. Therefore intrinsically motivated individuals will work on a problem because the challenge of providing a solution provides a sense of pleasure. Intrinsic motivation does not mean that a person will not seek rewards. It just means that such external rewards are not enough to keep them motivated. E.g. an intrinsically motivated team member will want to be paid highly for their work. However, if the work does not interest them the possibility of high pay is not enough to maintain that team members motivation to put the effort into the project.

Examples of intrinsic motivators:

- Challenge and responsibility, Flexibility, Stable work environment, Professional development, Peer recognition, Stimulating colleagues and managers, Exciting job content, Organisational culture, Location and community.

Herzberg refers to these as positive motivators. These are aspects of the job that deliver job satisfaction; thus these are the reasons why people want to undertake a particular task of job. Motivation therefore is about understanding what an individuals values i.e. what drives them and leveraging that for the benefit of the project, task or organisation.

Motivation in a project management context:

- Incentives and threats are invariably used with suppliers and contractors i.e. bonus payments for early delivery and liquidated damages for being late.
- Incentives and threats may also be applied to a project team although the project manager may not have the power to influence team members pay or the rewards available i.e. company car.

Often project managers have limited authority over staff - the power to remove or fire team members, to raise salary, award bonuses is kept by functional managers to whom the project team members have first allegiance. Therefore the project manager will sell, negotiate, persuade and tap into team members intrinsic motivators to get the best out of the team.

Frederick Herzberg: Motivation - Hygiene Theory (also known as Herzberg's Two Factor Theory)

Considered the pioneer of "job enrichment", Herzberg is regarded as one of the original thinkers in management and motivational theory. His theory shows that satisfaction and dissatisfaction at work nearly always arose from different factors and were not simply opposing reactions to the same factors.

The fundamental part of this theory can be gleaned from the following quote:

"We can expand ... by stating that the job satisfiers deal with the factors involved in doing the job, whereas the job dissatisfiers deal with the factors which define the job context." Herzberg 1959

So according to Herzberg, man has two sets of needs; one as an animal to avoid pain (hygiene needs i.e. food, warmth, shelter, safety etc.) and two as a human being to grow psychologically (motivational needs i.e. self development).

Examples of Herzberg hygiene needs (or maintenance factors or factors for dissatisfaction) in the work place:

● Policy, Relationship with supervisor, Work Conditions, Salary, Company Car, Status, Security, Relationship with Subordinates, Personal Life.

Herzberg's research identified that true motivators (or factors for satisfaction) were completely different factors:

● Achievement, Recognition, Work itself, Responsibility, Advancement.

So the factors that lead to job satisfaction are separate and distinct from those that lead to job dissatisfaction. In eliminating these you create peace not satisfaction which does not necessarily correlate with improved performance. When dissatisfiers are dealt with, there is neither dissatisfaction nor satisfaction therefore in order to motivate, the satisfiers also have to be present i.e. achievement, recognition responsibility etc.

To apply Herzberg's theory one needs to adopt a two stage process to motivate. First the elimination of dissatisfactions and second the assistance to find satisfactions.

The theory demonstrated the importance of psychological growth as a basic condition for lasting job satisfaction. Its relevance to project management is that often the main motivators available to a project manager are Herzberg's true motivators - those that develop job satisfaction - aren't we lucky!

Chapter 24 - Leadership

Assessment Criteria - assessment will require a learner to demonstrate that they can:

10.1 define leadership

10.2 outline how a project team leader can influence team performance

24.1 Leadership

Leadership is the ability to establish vision and direction, to influence and align others towards a common purpose, and to empower and inspire people to achieve project success. (BoK 6)

This definition consists of three linked parts - set the direction, align people in this direction and finally equip and inspire them to move in that direction. All these three parts are important.

Styles of leadership

Power and authority are generally expressed through leadership styles. Leadership style is the manner and approach of providing direction, implementing plans and motivating people. Effective leaders tend to employ more than one of these styles. However, most leaders tend to have a dominant style which is likely to be based on a combination of their values, beliefs and preferences. The early research (Kurt Lewin et al, 1939) identified three styles:

1. Authoritarian or Autocratic

In autocratic leadership, a leader exerts high levels of power over his or her employees or team members. Those within the team are given very few opportunities for making suggestions, even when these are in the team's/organisations interest. Most people tend to resent being treated this way. Thus, autocratic leadership tends to lead to high levels of absenteeism and staff turnover. Output does not benefit from the creativity and experience of team members therefore many of the benefits of teamwork are lost. There are situations where this style remains effective as the advantages of control outweigh the disadvantages. For example during controversy or crisis the organisation may require a strong leader who will tell them what to do. Or where employees require close supervision to perform certain tasks as in the case of routine or unskilled jobs.

2. Participative or Democratic

Democratic leaders make the final decision. However, they invite members of the team/organisation to contribute to the decision making process. This tends to increase job satisfaction as employees/team members are involved. This process also helps in the development of people skills. The involvement of employees/team members aids motivation as they feel in control. Participation takes time therefore tends to lead to things happening more slowly than the autocratic approach. However, the end result is better. This type of leadership is best employed in situations where team work and quality are more important than speed or productivity.

3. Delegative or Permissive (Laissez-faire)

This minimises the leader's involvement in decision-making allowing team-member/ organisation to make their own decisions, although the leader is ultimately responsible for the outcome. This can be effective if the leader monitors what is being achieved and communicates this to the team/organisation regularly. This works best when people are capable and motivated in making their own decisions or highly experienced therefore require little/no supervision to obtain the expected outcome and/or where there is little requirement for central coordination. e.g. sharing resources across a range of different people/groups. Unfortunately, it can also refer to situations where leaders are not exerting sufficient control. This can be infuriating where work requires coordination, active support and direction.

These three styles have the following drawback and benefits:

Autocratic: benefits - single-mindedness, speed and clarity particularly when a firm direction is required; drawbacks - not conducive to a team environment/productivity as team members are unable to contribute ideas or information.

Democratic: benefits - everyone contributes skills or talents therefore tends to lead to more work of a higher quality. Encourages staff development; drawbacks - the speed of this process tends to be slow and can frustrate the more action-oriented team members.

Permissive: benefits - best in a highly creative environment where people respond well to structure-free environment. Also effective when little/no group coordination required; drawbacks - Can be a sign of ineffective leadership as leader unwilling to exert control. These leaders can cause colleagues to accept inactivity as they avoid giving direction and guidance.

For fun, try allocating Prime Ministers into these styles.

24.2 Situational Leadership Model (Hersey and Blanchard)

An effective leader usually switches between styles according to the people they are dealing with. This type of leadership is call situational leadership. The situational approach to leadership emphasizes the authority of knowledge as the situation determines who should lead. In other word authority flows from the one who knows. So leadership can pass between the members of the group/organisation according to the situation. Situation in this context means primarily the task of the group.

Hersey and Blanchard proposed an analysis of the situation you are in which enables you to ascertain the appropriate leadership style. This model is dependent upon the team/organisation competencies in their task areas and commitment to their task. Situational leadership allows for your leadership style to vary from person to person or to vary with the same person.

Hersey and Blanchard characterised leadership as the amount of direction and support the leader is required to give to team/organisation members, depending on their level of maturity:

- **M1** - They still lack the specific skills required for the job in hand and are unable and unwilling to do or to take responsibility for this job or task. (According to Ken Blanchard "The honeymoon is over")/

- **M2** - They are unable to take on responsibility for the task being done; however, they are willing to work at the task. They are novice but enthusiastic.

- **M3** - They are experienced and able to do the task but lack the confidence or the willingness to take on responsibility.

- **M4** - They are experienced at the task, and comfortable with their own ability to do it well. They are able and willing to not only do the task, but to take responsibility for the task.

Behaviour of the leader

Each style corresponds to the equivalent maturity level ie S1 to M1.

S1 - Directing/Telling

This has a high task focus with a low relationship focus. Therefore the leader defines the roles and the task for team/organisation member and supervises them closely. Decisions are made by the leader and announced therefore communication is largely one way. In this is scenario the team/organisation lacks competence usually high on enthusiasm and commitment. Thus need direction and supervision to get started.

S2 - Coaching/Selling

This has a high task focus with a high relationship focus. Roles and tasks are still defined by the leader. However, will seek ideas/suggestions from team/organisation member. Decisions still leaders prerogative. Communication is more two way. In this scenario the team/organisation has some competence but lack commitment. Therefore need direction and supervision as still relatively inexperienced. They will also need support and praise to build self-esteem, involvement in decision making as these restore commitment.

S3 - Supporting/Participating

This has a low task focus with a high relationship focus. Day-to-day decisions such as task allocation and processes are delegated. Leader facilitates and takes part in decisions however, control is with the team/organisation. In this scenario the team/organisation has the competence but may lack confidence or motivation. So there is no need for direction because of skill however require support to bolster confidence and motivation.

S4 - Delegating/Empowering

This has a low task focus with a low relationship focus. Leaders are still involved in decisions and problem-solving. However, control is with the team/organisation. The team/organisation decides how and when the leader will be involved. In this scenario the team/organisation have both competence and commitment. There is very little need for supervision or support as they are willing and able to work on the project by themselves.

24.3 Leadership Characteristics

The following characteristics have been identified by the APM as important in project management (see section 7.7 of the APM BoK 5)

Open and positive attitude, Common Sense, Open minded, Adaptability, Inventiveness, Prudent risk taker, Fairness, Commitment.

Another list appears in 'Project Management' by Lester (5th edition 2007)

Adaptability, Attitude, Charisma, Cognitive ability, Commitment, Common sense, Creativity, Drive, Fairness, Flexibility, Honesty, Integrity, Intelligence, Open-mindedness, Prudence, Self-confidence, Technical knowledge

In his book, The Leader's Code (2013), Donovan Campbell writes that the best and most effective leaders are those who practice kindness regularly and intentionally; an unexpected comment from a former captain in the US Marine Corps who served in Iraq. Over time they produce the best and most effective teams. His six key attributes are humility, excellence, kindness, discipline, courage, wisdom.

Whilst there are overlaps between these lists, they encourage recall of comments by Peter Drucker in his book, Managing for the Future (1992),

"Leadership ... has little to do with 'leadership qualities' and even less to do with 'charisma'. Its essence is performance."

"The foundation of effective leadership is thinking through the organisation's mission, defining it and establishing it, clearly and visibly." This takes one back to the APM definition of leadership with which we started this chapter.

APM Sample Paper

Question - 16

Chapter 25 - Teamwork

Assessment Criteria - assessment will require a learner to demonstrate that they can:

10.3 define what is meant by the term project team

10.4 outline the advantages and disadvantages of team models such as Belbin and Margerison McCann

25.1 Teamwork

A project team is a group of people who are responsible to the project manager for working together to achieve the objectives. For some projects, the individuals are responsible for particular work packages within the Work Breakdown Structure.

In essence, each person in the team puts aside his or her individual needs to work towards the larger group objective. The interactions among the members and the work they complete is called teamwork.

Teamwork is a group of people working in collaboration or by cooperation towards a common goal. (BoK 6)

Collaboration = Co-labour - work alongside on single shared goal - united effort to solve problem.

Cooperation = Co-operate - perform together on single shared tasks that contribute to the whole.

This highlights one of the big problems of team selection - do you go for the best players (who cooperate) or those who make up the best team (collaborate) - see numerous discussions over the composition of the England football team!

25.2 Margerison-McCann Model

Team Management Systems (TMS) was established in 1985 by Dr Margerison and Dr McCann to commercialise the Team Performance Wheel.

The TMS approach focuses on identifying and understanding key work elements that prove to be a reliable and valid focus in explaining why some individuals, teams, and organisations perform, work effectively and achieve their objectives, while others fail. These functions are activities that take place within teams.

There are close similarities with the Belbin team roles, but they are not identical. The underlying system is based on the Jungian Type Inventory.

Role	Description
Reporter-Adviser	Likes to help others. Gathers information and makes it understandable. Listens patiently before deciding. Prefers to be slow and fully right rather than quick and mostly right.
Creator-Innovator	Likes independence to think and innovate. Not afraid to challenge norms. Good at starting new things.
Explorer-Promoter	Likes to connect with people outside the group as well as inside. Good at seeing the big picture. Good at creating enthusiasm for new ideas.
Assessor-Developer	Likes experimenting with new ideas. Good at evaluating different options. Good at organising new activities.
Thruster-organisers	Likes 'making things happen'. May be impatient. Ready to add energy and turn an idea into an action.
Concluder-producer	Likes completing things on time, on budget and to specification. Likes using well-developed skills. Good at methodical, careful work.
Controller-inspector	Likes working with detailed information. Good with facts and figures.
Upholder-maintainer	Looks after the physical and social elements of the team. A great source of emotional strength for others on the team. May have strong views on how the team should be run.

25.3 Belbin Team Roles

Belbin first began studying teams of students at Henley Management College in the 1970s. Over a period of ten years, he carried out extended observational research to determine which factors influenced team failure or success. His teams of students (maybe 10-11 executives) each week tackled a task and reported back at the end of the week.

At first, Belbin hypothesised that high-intellect teams would succeed where lower-intellect teams would not. However, the outcome of this research was that certain teams, predicted to be excellent based on intellect, failed to fulfil their potential. In fact, it became apparent by looking at the various combinations that it was not intellect, but balance, which enabled a team to succeed - **"Teams are a question of balance"**.

Thus one has to work out the correct balance of required roles for each project. Project management is usually about working out the right balance that suits a project, in direct contrast to application of a set of rules.

The most successful teams tended to be those with a mix of different people, i.e. those with a range of different behaviours.

Originally published with eight roles, a ninth role - the specialist - was added later. The role was not revealed in the original research because no specialised knowledge was required for the simulation exercise. These nine roles can be put into three categories:

Thinking and problem solving roles:

Team Role	Contribution	Allowable weakness
Plant	Creative, imaginative, unorthodox. Solves difficult problems. Plants tend to be concerned with major issues rather than with details. Tends to have radical approaches to team functioning and problems. These are ideas people that tend to have a high IQ. They are usually introverted whilst also dominant and original.	Ignores incidentals. Too preoccupied to communicate effectively. Tend to disregard practical details and can be argumentative.

Team Role	Contribution	Allowable weakness
Monitor Evaluator	Objective judgement, sober strategic and discerning. Sees all options. Judges accurately. These are judicious, prudent, intelligent people with a low need to achieve. Monitor evaluators contribute at times of crucial decision making as they are capable of evaluating competing proposals. They tend not to be deflected by emotional arguments, are serious minded, take time to come to decisions as they need to think things over. Take pride in never being wrong.	Lack drive and ability to inspire others. Can appear boring or over critical. Tend to be in high level appointments.
Specialist	Single-minded, self-starting and dedicated. Provides knowledge and skills. Tend to be introverted and anxious. Usually dedicated and committed.	Contributes on a narrow front. Dwells on technicalities. Single-mindedness and a lack of interest in other peoples' subjects.

Action oriented roles:

Team Role	Contribution	Allowable weakness
Shaper	Challenging, dynamic, thrives on pressure. The drive and courage to overcome obstacles. The shaper is a tasks focused leader with lots of nervous energy, who has a high motivation to achieve and for whom winning is the name of the game. The shaper is committed to achieving ends and will "shape" others into achieving the aims of the team.	Prone to provocation, offends others feelings. They challenge, argue or disagree, and will display aggression in the pursuit of goal achievement. The presence of two or three shapers in a team can lead to conflict, aggravation and infighting.

Team Role	Contribution	Allowable weakness
Implemen ter	Disciplined, reliable, conservative and efficient. Turns ideas into practical actions. Implementers are aware of external obligations and are disciplined, conscientious and have a good self-image. They tend to be tough-minded and practical, trusting and tolerant, respecting established traditions. They are characterised by low anxiety and tend to work for the team in a practical and realistic way. Implementers feature prominently in positions of responsibility in large organisations. They tend to do the jobs that others do not want to do and do them well. E.g. disciplining employees.	Inflexible, conservative and slow to respond to new possibilities.
Completer Finisher	Conscientious, painstaking, anxious. Searches out errors and omissions. Delivers on time. Completer finishers give attention to detail, aims to complete and to do so throughly. They make steady effort and are consistent in their work. Generally not interested in the glamour of spectacular success.	Inclined to worry unduly, reluctant to delegate.

People oriented roles:

Team Role	Contribution	Allowable weakness
Coordinat or	Mature, confident, a good chairperson. Clarifies goals, promotes decision-making, delegates well. The coordinator is a person-oriented leader. This person is trusting, accepting, dominant and is committed to team goals and objectives. The coordinator is a positive thinker who approves of goal attainment, struggle and effort in others. The coordinator is someone who is tolerant always listens to others, but strong enough to reject their advice.	Can often be seen as manipulative. Off-loads personal work. May not stand out in a team and usually does not have a sharp intellect.

Team Role	Contribution	Allowable weakness
Team-worker	Cooperative, mild, perceptive and diplomatic. Listens, builds, averts friction. Team workers make helpful interventions to avert potential friction and enable difficult characters within the team to use their skills to positive ends. They keep team spirit up and allow other members to contribute effectively. Their diplomatic skills together with their sense of humour are assets to a team. They have skills in listening, coping with awkward people and are sociable sensitive and people oriented.	Indecisive in crunch situations. So are indecisive in moments of crisis and reluctant to do things that might hurt others.
Resource Investigator	Extrovert, enthusiastic, communicative. Explores opportunities. Develops contacts. The resource investigator is the executive who is never in their office. The resource investigator explores opportunity and develops contacts. Resource investigators are good negotiators who probe others for information and support. Will pick up other's ideas and develop them. They are characterised by sociability and enthusiasm are good at liaison work and exploring resources outside the team.	Over-optimistic. Loses interest once initial enthusiasm has passed. Is usually not the source of original ideas.

Applications

Belbin's approach can be used to allocate roles in a team or project. It enables motivation of team members as they are normally allowed to perform activities that interest them. It can lead to balanced teams therefore reduces risk and requires less management attention. Note that Belbin lists allowable weaknesses in the team roles.

Limitations

The model is subjective as it is based on self-perception. We do not see ourselves as others see us. Represents tasks and functions in the self-management of activities in a team and are not personality types. Does not account for hierarchal relations between people.

APM Sample Paper

Question - 46

Appendix 1 - Syllabus learning outcomes and assessment criteria

Introductory Certificate

The APM Project Fundamentals Qualification

Syllabus, learning outcomes and assessment criteria
aligned to the *APM Body of Knowledge 6th edition*

Syllabus learning outcomes and assessment criteria

Learning outcomes	Assessment criteria
When awarded credit for this unit, a learner will:	**Assessment of this learning outcome will require a learner to demonstrate that they can:**
1 Understand project management and the operating environment	1.1 define a project
	1.2 identify the differences between a project and business as usual
	1.3 define project management
	1.4 state the key purpose of project management
	1.5 list the core components of project management
	1.6 list the benefits to an organisation of effective project management
	1.7 define programme and portfolio management and their relationship with project management
	1.8 define the term project environment
	1.9 define the components of the PESTLE acronym
2 Understand the project lifecycle	2.1 define the term project life cycle
	2.2 state the phases of a typical project life cycle
	2.3 identify reasons for structuring projects into phases
3 Understand the management structure by which projects operate	3.1 define the roles and responsibilities of
	• project manager
	• project sponsor
	• project steering group/ board
	• project team members
	• project office
	• end users

Continued

4. Understand project management planning	4.1 state the main purpose of a project management plan
	4.2 define who is involved in the creation of the project management plan
	4.3 explain why the project management plan needs to be approved, owned and shared
	4.4 identify the purpose and the typical content of a business case
	4.5 define the role of the sponsor and project manager in relation to the business case
	4.6 define stakeholders and stakeholder management and explain why stakeholder analysis is important.
	4.7 define benefits management
	4.8 define the use of KPIs
	4.9 identify typical estimating methods (including analytical, comparative, parametric)
	4.10 describe the estimating funnel
	4.11 define success criteria in the context of managing projects
	4.12 identify typical success factors that may contribute to successful projects
	4.13 define the purpose and benefits of project reporting
5. Understand project scope management	5.1 define project scope management
	5.2 describe how product breakdown structure {PBS} and work breakdown structure {WBS} are used to illustrate the scope of work required
	5.3 define the uses of
	• Cost Breakdown Structure {CBS}
	• Organisational Breakdown Structure {OBS}
	• Responsibility Assignment Matrix {RAM}
	5.4 define the following in relation to scope management
	• configuration management
	• change control
	5.5 explain the relationship between change control and configuration management
	5.6 list the steps involved in a typical change control process
	5.7 list the activities in a typical configuration management process
6. Understand scheduling and resource management	6.1 identify the purpose of scheduling
	6.2 outline different approaches to scheduling (including critical path analysis, total float, Gantt(bar)charts, baseline, milestone)
	6.3 define resource management
	6.4 define procurement within the context of project management
	6.5 list different categories and types of resources needed for projects

Continued

7. Understand risk management and issue management	7.1 define risk
	7.2 define risk management
	7.3 explain the purpose of risk management
	7.4 outline a high level risk management process
	7.5 describe the use of a risk register
	7.6 define an issue
	7.7 define issue management
	7.8 explain the difference between an issue and a risk
	7.9 describe the use of an issue log
8. Understand project quality management	8.1 define quality
	8.2 define quality management
	8.3 define the following: quality planning, quality assurance, quality control and continual improvement
	8.4 outline the difference between quality control and quality assurance

	8.5 identify the purpose of:
	    ▪ gate reviews
	    ▪ post project reviews
	    ▪ benefit reviews
	    ▪ peer reviews
	    ▪ project audits

9. Understand communication in the project environment	9.1 define communication
	9.2 outline different media of communication identify potential barriers to effective communication
	9.3 identify ways to facilitate effective communication
	9.4 define the contents of a communication plan
	9.5 explain the benefits of a communication plan
10. Understand principles of leadership and teamwork	10.1 define leadership
	10.2 outline how a project team leader can influence team performance
	10.3 define what is meant by the term project team
	10.4 outline the advantages and disadvantages of team models such as Belbin and Margerison McCann

Appendix 2 - Assessment criteria matched to chapter

Chapter	Topic	Assessment Criteria
	Project context	
1	Introduction to the course	
2	Projects and project management	1.1, 1.2, 1.3, 1.4, 1.5, 1.6
3	Programme and portfolio management	1.7
4	Project life cycles	2.1, 2.2, 2.3
	Core Business Case	
5	What the project is	4.11, 4.8, 4.12
6	Benefits - why the project should go ahead	4.7
7	Estimating costs for cost/benefit analysis	4.9(part)
8	Environment and stakeholders	1.8, 1.9, 4.6
9	Uncertainties in benefits and costs - risks	7.1, 7.2, 7.3, 7.4, 7.5
	Planning and control	
10	Full business case and project management plan	4.4, 4.5, 4.1, 4.2, 4.3
11	Quality management	8.1, 8.2, 8.3, 8.4
12	Reviews	8.5
13	Scope management - breakdown structures	5.1, 5.2, 5.3
14	Estimating	4.9(part), 4.10
15	Scheduling	6.1, 6.2
16	Resource management and procurement	6.3, 6.5, 6.4
17	Issues and change control	7.6, 7.7, 7.8, 7.9, 5.4(part), 5.6
18	Configuration management	5.4(part), 5.5, 5.7
19	Information management and reporting	4.13

Chapter	Topic	Assessment Criteria
	People - interactions, organisation and skills	
20	Communication	9.1, 9.2, 9.3, 9.4, 9.5
21	Roles and responsibilities	3.1
22	What makes a good Project Manager?	-
23	Motivation	-
24	Leadership	10.1, 10.2
25	Teamwork	10.3, 10.4

Appendix 3 - APM Sample Paper - answers may be found on the APM website at www.apm.org.uk/

1. **A communication management plan identifies the relevant information that should be communicated to:**

   a. the project team.
   b. the project stakeholders.
   c. the project board.
   d. the project sponsor.

2. **Which one of the following statements is <u>true</u>?**

   a. Independent reviews and quality audits form part of quality assurance to ensure the project manager delivers on time and to budget.
   b. Quality assurance provides confidence to stakeholders that requirements for quality will be exceeded.
   c. Quality control verifies that the project deliverables conform to specification, are fit for purpose and meet stakeholder expectations.
   d. Quality planning enables the project manager to manage the trade-off between customer expectations and budget.

3. **Project risk management is <u>best</u> described as:**

   a. managing responses to threats.
   b. identifying and acknowledging threats and opportunities.
   c. planning responses to threats.
   d. minimising threats and maximising opportunities.

4. **Which one of the following <u>best</u> describes a project issue?**

   a. A major problem that requires formal escalation.
   b. A problem that the project manager has to deal with on a day-to-day basis.
   c. An uncertain event that may or may not occur.
   d. An opportunity that occurs through change control.

5. **Scheduling can <u>best</u> be defined as the process used to determine:**

   a. overall project duration.
   b. project cost estimating.
   c. the project management plan.
   d. sub-contractor's responsibilities.

6. **Which one of the following statements is <u>true</u>?**

   a. An increase in project scope is likely to increase project cost.
   b. A decrease in the project time is likely to increase project quality.
   c. An increase in the project quality requirements is likely to decrease project cost.
   d. A decrease in the project cost is likely to decrease project time.

7. **Which one of the following statements <u>best</u> defines the purpose of a Product Breakdown Structure (PBS)?**

   a. To define the hierarchy of deliverables that are required to be produced on the project.
   b. To define how the products are produced by identifying derivations and dependencies.
   c. To establish the extent of work required prior to project commissioning and the handover.
   d. To identify the health and safety strategies and procedures to be used on the project.

8. Which one of the following is <u>least</u> likely to be a success criteria?

    a. A target for the project to receive zero change requests.
    b. The date by which the project is to be completed.
    c. Delivery of products that meet required specifications.
    d. The awarding of bonuses to senior management.

9. Which one of the following is a <u>valid</u> project Key Performance Indicator (KPI)?

    a. Staff appraisals.
    b. Management buy in.
    c. Milestone achievement.
    d. Master schedule.

10. Which one of the following statements is <u>true</u>?

    a. The business case is owned by the sponsor and is created during the concept phase of the project life cycle.
    b. The business case is owned by the project manager and is created during the concept phase of the project life cycle.
    c. The business case is owned by the sponsor and is created during definition phase of the project life cycle.
    d. The business case is owned by the project manager and is created during the definition phase of the project life cycle.

11. Who owns the Project Management Plan (PMP)?

    a. The project team.
    b. The chief executive.
    c. The project manager.
    d. The project support office.

12. Which one of the following <u>best</u> describes users?

    a. Providers of both strategic and tactical direction to the project.
    b. Those intended to receive benefits or operate outputs.
    c. Facilitators of an appropriate issue resolution procedure.
    d. Those providing full-time commitment to the project.

13. Which statement <u>best</u> describes a responsibility of the project manager:

    a. to be the sole source of expertise for estimating techniques on cost and time.
    b. to deliver the project objectives to enable benefits to be realised.
    c. to take ultimate accountability for the delivery of the business benefits.
    d. to delegate all accountability for managing time, cost and quality to team leaders.

14. A project is <u>typically</u> defined in terms of scope, time, cost and which other parameter?

    a. Benefits.
    b. Quality.
    c. Tolerance.
    d. Controls.

15. Which one of the following statements is <u>true</u>?

    a. Business-as-usual activities cannot be improved.
    b. Business-as-usual activities are more difficult to manage than projects.
    c. Projects are transient endeavours that bring about change to business-as-usual.
    d. A project is always the starting point for operation refinement.

16. What is defined as "the ability to influence and align others towards a common purpose"?

    a. Teamwork.
    b. Motivation.
    c. Management.
    d. Leadership.

17. Which one is a <u>true</u> statement relating to project communications?

    a. A project sponsor is responsible for all communication methods and media.
    b. Different stakeholders typically have different communication needs.
    c. It is best to have a standard set of project reports used for every project.
    d. Email is the only way to communicate with large numbers of people.

18. In project management, the term quality is <u>best</u> defined as:

    a. inspection, testing and measurement.
    b. reviews and audits.
    c. fitness for purpose of deliverables.
    d. professionally-bound project reports.

19. The <u>main</u> outcome of risk identification, in a risk management process, is to:

    a. identify and determine the relative importance of the project risks.
    b. identify and describe all risks that might occur on the project.
    c. identify and determine the responses to the project risks.
    d. identify and describe risks that have occurred on previous projects.

20. Which one of the following is <u>not</u> considered in resource management?

    a. Identifying resources.
    b. Influencing resources.
    c. Assigning resources to activities.
    d. Matching resources to the schedule.

21. Which one of the following does project change control <u>primarily</u> seek to ensure?

    a. All variance to the project scope is evaluated.
    b. No reduction in the perceived quality of the project outcome.
    c. Management costs of the project do not increase.
    d. Any decrease in the scoped deliverable of the project is rejected.

22. Which one of the following is captured in the Work Breakdown Structure (WBS)?

a. The life cycle phases.
b. The logical order of tasks.
c. The scope of the project.
d. Project costs.

23. Project reporting can best be defined as:

a. informing stakeholders about the project.
b. storing and archiving of project information.
c. gathering stakeholder feedback.
d. collecting project information.

24. Which one of the following statements best defines an estimate?

a. An approximation of project time and cost targets, refined throughout the project life cycle.
b. A prediction of a future condition or event based on information or knowledge available now.
c. The value of useful work done at any given point in a project to give a measure of progress.
d. A situation that affects or influences the outcome of the project expressed in time or cost terms.

25. The justification for the investment to be made in a project is documented in the:

a. Cost Breakdown Structure.
b. procurement strategy.
c. business case.
d. Project Management Plan.

26. Which one of the following is a responsibility of the project steering group/board?

a. To identify potential problems for the project team to solve.
b. To provide strategic direction and guidance to the sponsor.
c. To manage the project team in all daily activities.
d. To receive and consider daily reports from team members.

27. One of the reasons a project life cycle is split into phases is to:

a. facilitate formal go/no-go decision making during the project.
b. balance the costs of work in each phase of project development.
c. mirror the major deployments of resources throughout the project.
d. chunk work into time periods of similar durations.

28. Which of the following best describes a project environment?

a. The type of organisation concerned with implementation.
b. The structured method used to control the project.
c. The context within which a project is undertaken.
d. An understanding of the risks involved in the project.

Introductory Certificate – the APM Project Fundamentals Qualification. Exam paper

29. Which one of the following statements **best** describes a project?

    a. A project is a set of tools and techniques often used when delivering organisational change.
    b. A project is the sum of activities needed to remove uncertainty from a unique piece of work.
    c. A unique transient endeavour undertaken to achieve a desired outcome.
    d. A project is a method of planning work.

30. The document that identifies what information needs to be shared, to whom, why, when and how is called the:

    a. communication management plan.
    b. stakeholder mapping grid.
    c. document distribution schedule.
    d. responsibility assignment matrix.

31. An important aim of a post-project review is to:

    a. validate overall progress to date against the budget and schedule.
    b. capture learning and document it for future usage.
    c. ensure acceptance of all permanent documentation, signed by the sponsor.
    d. establish that project benefits have been identified.

32. The process that evaluates overall project performance to provide confidence is called:

    a. quality assurance.
    b. quality planning.
    c. quality control.
    d. quality audit.

33. Which one of the following statements about the project risk register is **false**?

    a. It facilitates the review and monitoring of risks.
    b. It facilitates the risk appetite.
    c. It facilitates the recording of risk responses.
    d. It facilitates the recording of risks.

34. Which one of the following statements **best** defines procurement?

    a. A technique to establish the best approach for obtaining the resources for the project.
    b. A group of interrelated resources and activities that transform inputs into outputs.
    c. The description of the purpose, form and components to support delivery of a product.
    d. The process by which products and services required for the project are acquired.

35. Once a change has been requested what is the next step in the change control process?

    a. Evaluate the change.
    b. Advise the sponsor.
    c. Update the change log.
    d. Update the project plan.

36. A Responsibility Assignment Matrix (RAM) can be used to:

    a. define the terms of reference of the project manager.
    b. define the limits of the project sponsor's responsibilities.
    c. allocate risk management response activities to project personnel.
    d. allocate work packages to those responsible for project work.

37. An Organisational Breakdown Structure (OBS) is used to identify:

    a. the reporting structure and current availability of all individuals in the project.
    b. technical ability and line of communication for all individuals in the project.
    c. lines of communication and responsibility for all the individual managers in the project.
    d. the reporting structure and lines of communication for all individuals in the projects.

38. Which one of the following best describes project success criteria?

    a. Actively seeking some senior management support.
    b. Measures by which the success of the project is judged.
    c. Achievement of milestones.
    d. A motivated project team.

39. Comparative estimating uses:

    a. current data from similar projects.
    b. historic data from all projects.
    c. historic data from similar projects.
    d. current data from all projects.

40. Which one of the following best describes a project stakeholder?

    a. A party who is concerned about the project going ahead.
    b. A party with an interest or role in the project or is impacted by the project.
    c. A party who has a vested interest in the outcome of the project.
    d. A party who has a financial stake in the organisation managing the project.

41. The main purpose of the Project Management Plan is to:

    a. provide justification for undertaking the project in terms of evaluating the benefit, cost and risk of alternative options.
    b. ensure the project sponsor has tight control of the project manager's activity.
    c. document the outcomes of the planning process and provide the reference document for managing the project.
    d. document the outcome of the risk, change and configuration management processes.

42. Who has ultimate responsibility for project risk?

    a. Steering group.
    b. Risk owner.
    c. Project sponsor.
    d. Project manager.

Introductory Certificate – the APM Project Fundamentals Qualification. Exam paper

43. **When a project has completed the handover and closure phase:**

    a. the project deliverables are ready for commissioning.
    b. the project deliverables are ready for handing over to the users.
    c. the project documentation must be disposed of.
    d. the capability is now in place for the benefits to be realised.

44. **Which one of the following illustrates why effective project management is beneficial to an organisation?**

    a. It utilises resources as and when required under direction of a project manager.
    b. It advocates employing a consultancy firm which specialises in managing change.
    c. It recommends using only highly skilled people in the project team.
    d. It ensures that the chief executive is accountable for the achievement of the defined benefits.

45. **A <u>key</u> aspect of managing a project involves:**

    a. defining which operational systems to put in place.
    b. identifying routine tasks.
    c. ensuring ongoing operations are maintained.
    d. planning to achieve defined objectives.

46. **Which one of the following statements <u>best</u> defines teamwork?**

    a. People working collaboratively towards a common goal.
    b. Developing skills that will enhance project performance.
    c. Gathering the right people together to work on a project.
    d. Establishing vision and direction towards a common purpose.

47. **A review undertaken to decide whether a project should proceed into its next phase is known as a:**

    a. gate review.
    b. feasibility study.
    c. milestone review.
    d. evaluation review.

48. **Which one of the following statements <u>best</u> describes the use of an issue log?**

    a. A summary of all possible alternative resolutions of an issue.
    b. A summary of all the project issues, their analysis and status.
    c. A tool to ensure that a process is in place for capturing all issues.
    d. A tool to ensure that the issue management process is adhered to.

49. **The <u>main</u> aim of a project risk management process should be to:**

    a. identify project risks and then manage them appropriately.
    b. identify all project risks and transfer them immediately.
    c. identify all the things that are threats or opportunities on a project.
    d. satisfy the organisation's project management process.

50. **What is a visual representation of a project's planned activities against a calendar called?**

   a. A Gantt chart.
   b. A critical path network.
   c. A product flow diagram.
   d. A Pareto chart.

51. **Configuration management is <u>best</u> described as:**

   a. control in the implementation of changes to project schedules.
   b. an organisation to review proposed changes to the project deliverables.
   c. quality control of project deliverables and documentation.
   d. creation, maintenance and controlled change of the project deliverables.

52. **A Cost Breakdown Structure (CBS) shows costs assigned to:**

   a. individual work packages using the Work Breakdown Structure (WBS).
   b. individual resources using the Work Breakdown Structure (WBS).
   c. individual resources using the Responsibility Assignment Matrix (RAM).
   d. individual deliverables using the Responsibility Assignment Matrix (RAM)

53. **The accuracy of an estimate should:**

   a. decrease as a project progresses through its life cycle.
   b. increase as a project progresses through its life cycle.
   c. stay constant throughout the project life cycle.
   d. vary independently of where the project is in its life cycle.

54. **Which one of the following <u>best</u> defines a benefit?**

   a. A positive result of stakeholder management.
   b. The successful management of a project.
   c. An improvement resulting from project deliverables.
   d. The successful delivery of project reports and updates.

55. **Which one of the following is <u>true</u> for the Project Management Plan (PMP)?**

   a. The Project Management Plan is developed by the project manager and team and owned by the sponsor.
   b. A draft of the Project Management Plan is developed by the sponsor at the same time as the business case.
   c. The Project Management Plan is developed by the sponsor and owned by the project manager.
   d. The Project Management Plan is developed by the project manager and team and owned by the project manager.

56. **Who are project team members <u>primarily</u> accountable to?**

   a. External stakeholders.
   b. The end users.
   c. The finance director.
   d. The project manager.

57. The phases of a project life cycle are:

a. starting, planning, control and closing.
b. concept, definition, development, handover and closure.
c. initiation, definition, planning, monitoring and operations.
d. concept, definition, implementation and operations.

58. A portfolio can <u>best</u> be defined as:

a. a group of projects and programmes carried out within an organisation.
b. a group of programmes carried out under the sponsorship of an organisation.
c. a group of projects carried out under the sponsorship of an organisation.
d. a range of products and services offered by an organisation.

59. Which one of the following <u>best</u> describes project management?

a. Using APM's *Body of Knowledge 6th edition* as a guide to all projects.
b. Employing a project manager who has undertaken similar projects.
c. Utilising team members who can work on a project full time.
d. Application of processes and methods throughout the project life cycle.

60. Which structure shows the reporting relationships and communications channels for a project?

a. Work Breakdown Structure.
b. Organisational Breakdown Structure.
c. Product Breakdown Structure.
d. Responsibility assignment structure.